Christmas
1971

Max & Carolyn
from
Dad & Mom

Testimonies Of The Restoration

Testimonies Of The Restoration

Compiled by NORMAN D. RUOFF

A second volume of testimonies from the pages of the
Restoration Witness

Reorganized Church of Jesus Christ of Latter Day Saints

Preface

A world church—the dream of the persons who make up the body known as the Reorganized Church of Jesus Christ of Latter Day Saints—becomes reality as people from all over that world testify of the goodness of God, heartbreaks which become strengths, and the courage to stand for that which is worthwhile.

It is presumed that those who have experiences change and become more vital to the growth of the church. It is also presumed that those who read the testimonies of others also change and become more loving and more efficient in ministering. This is the way of the Christ: to learn of him and be transformed into right beings.

As editor of the *Restoration Witness* I have met vicariously many people. They have shared with me their feelings, and I believe they use their newfound faith or wisdom for the benefit of the kingdom. But even if they are poor stewards over the testimony which was given them the effect of the experience becomes valid to those who read and are transformed.

One young woman, a member but a skeptic, found strength on her hospital bed from one of the testimonies included in this collection and has been able to confront many additional problems since her release. A personal testimony once printed is no longer personal but if shared honestly is doing what it was meant to do in the first place: to minister. May the reader be stimulated to do good, to be open-minded with his fellowman, and to bear testimony of the love of God.

Norman D. Ruoff

Contents

You're a Good Man — The Lord Loves You

By Robert Matthews

The simplest statement in the world—short, terse—spoken by a church leader to a dazed and puzzled man ready for anything—anything, that is, but the full meaning of that important statement. No one had asked him to speak to me, and to my knowledge no one had told him of my problems; but now as I look back some years later, I'm sure that this sweet and meaningful message saved my life, perhaps physically, but surely spiritually.

I had been asked to serve our church college in public relations and fund-raising. I had always considered myself something of a student; however, I was unprepared for what had happened to me as a young, unsophisticated student from high school. I'm not sure when the trouble began, but at some time in my life the dazzling world of inquiry had hit me and left me naked and scared just like many people much younger than I.

This was strange, however, for I'd been through the mill. I had read Schopenhauer and Nietzsche some time between the ages of 15 and 18. I had studied and read many of the odd mystical beliefs years before the army. I'd bombed and probably maimed and killed. I had joined the church and had been ordained. I'd served as pastor, teacher, and counselor; but suddenly, or not so suddenly, a dark gray world of doubt, a doubt about everything, literally tore my life to shreds—doubt about God, love, church, personal values, and home. You name it; I doubted it. I was left with no hope, no courage, and no self-respect. Through all this I had somehow lost sight of a sound marriage, a lovely home, and fine children; even these failed to supply that important something to give real meaning to life.

There had been many desperate efforts to find help—grasping at straws is a common habit of drowning men; but I found nothing but black, bleak fear and despair. Ministry became a sham, a pretense to hold those few important things together—home and children. Life itself became a burden from which to escape. How I yearned to somehow turn back the clock to a simple faith. And I asked over and over, How did all this come about? Most of my life had been centered around the Christian church. Somehow simple curiosity and a desire to know, the common disease (or hope) of all man, had crushed the very reason for intellectual search—the common denominator with eternity.

But I continued to grasp at straws. A simple invitation to a weekend retreat offered one more—not too important perhaps but nonetheless one more. The weekend had come and almost gone with nothing spectacular happening. During the final service I sat on the front row in a dull state. I was rather oblivious to what was being said. I was unaware that a friend who sat by my side was concerned and worried about me. But I had noticed that one of the church leaders sitting on the rostrum had looked my way several times. After the service the brother on the rostrum motioned to me that he wanted to see me. I walked forward and he looked me straight in the eye and said, "Bob, you're a good man. The Lord loves you." He said no more and I left with tears streaming down my face, but tears came easily in those days.

But like all revelation the full meaning of that phrase has gradually blossomed within my understanding. I say gradually because the full beauty of any meaningful phrase becomes an ever growing part of creation.

If God loved me and if he saw me as a good man, what else was there of basic importance? And, of course, the answer is *nothing;* absolutely nothing else really matters. If this basic and fundamental frame of reference was true, then I could doubt, fear, study, discard, or reshuffle all of belief and that one solid fact could hold as growth quietly and surely took place.

Suddenly all of life seemed different. The cold search for truth by way of doubt seemed bare and ridiculous, while at the same time the need to clutch fearfully at basic, unresearched, unevaluated beliefs became an unnecessary escape.

If God loves me, then salvation is really his problem, one somehow already answered very simply no matter how complex we may make it.

Since that Sunday, that Sunday so long ago, many wonderful things have happened. A new and wonderful feeling of personal worth has replaced the constant fear of failure and worthlessness. I am an object of love—a love so consuming and real that my many shortcomings and mistakes are constantly caught up in the marvelous reflection of his love and can be seen for what they really are—the necessary pain of growth that quietly, with unrelenting force, draws me to communion with him.

All mankind is irrevocably caught up in this same love—and until we see each other in the simple light of His love, we shall miss the true path to peace and freedom. Love is the essence of life.

God Had Gone Before

By Carole Ann Mead

When my husband told me that he had received orders for Italy I was thrilled beyond imagination. Three years in

Europe sounded wonderful, but there was no congregation of our church in Italy, and we would be isolated from the church again.

For two years we had been stationed in a town where we had attended a church mission of approximately forty people. My husband is a minister in our church, as well as a member of the Air Force. He was appointed pastor of the mission and was serving in this capacity when we received orders to move. How we hated to leave our good friends in the church—with only a hope of meeting church people during the next three years.

As we flew across the ocean, we also made plans to attend a military retreat held for members of our church stationed in Europe. The retreat is held each September at Berchtesgaden, Germany, a military recreation area. We attended the retreat just three months after arriving at our new base in Italy. Our spirits were lifted high and we looked forward with anticipation to the coming three years. Three years to get out those church books there had never been time to read! A chance to complete my compilation of a catalog of church camp songs. There now seemed to be time to do all the things we had wanted to do.

When we returned to Italy, we carried the spirit of the retreat with us. All too soon, however, this changed. We attended our base chapel, for there was no other church to attend, and held our Communion services in our home once a month. Our son had been baptized by his father in Berchtesgaden, so our Communion services were for the three of us with our two little girls as members of our "congregation." How different this was from what we had known before in our wonderful little mission back in the States. How we missed the Saints and yearned to be with them!

In my associations on the base I found that many people

had the attitude that they could not serve God in a chapel of all faiths. Many decided they would wait until they got back to the United States and work in their own faith. I couldn't imagine an attitude such as this, for God is everywhere.

In our adult Sunday school class I was shocked by such statements as "An evening at the club with drinking and dancing enhances my marriage." I had been away from attitudes such as this for a long time and had led a seemingly "sheltered" life since I had joined the church five years previously. These things were hard for me to face. I began to look for ways that I could serve; when I was asked to serve as women's leader, I readily accepted, hoping that in this way I might direct the thoughts and actions of some of God's children. It was quite a struggle.

When things seemed to be at their lowest, we received a letter from our church missionary in Germany telling my husband that he had been called to the office of elder. This is a priesthood office of greater responsibility than the office of priest which he held. My husband said to me, "What shall I do?" To make a decision such as this without counsel and without guidance was seemingly impossible. It had been eleven months since we had received church ministry or visited with the Saints. It had been eleven months since we had attended the last retreat. We felt such a great need to be "refilled" with the good Spirit which we had received before. The letter from Germany had stated that if my husband accepted this call, he would be ordained at the military retreat just twenty days hence. We, of course, turned to prayer and sought counsel from our heavenly Father.

During this time of decision and prayer another pitfall occurred. One of the chaplains, who had just been transferred to our base, preached a sermon in which he told us that God did not care for us as individuals and that it was fruitless to pray, for He wouldn't answer the prayers of individuals. What a thing to hear when we were trying to make the decision to serve Him in a greater capacity and depending on His aid in making the decision.

This was the most difficult thing I had had to face. How could I accept ministry for two years from a chaplain like this? Such loneliness had built up within me over the months that I feared I was not susceptible to God's answers anymore. Surely I had prayed! Surely I had dwelled with Him over these months of isolation, for He had been my strength! I seemed not to have any strength left. I felt that when I was in the company of the Saints again at our retreat all would be restored in me and I would be strong again.

This restoration was not to happen immediately. As we arrived at the retreat and I mingled with the Saints, my heart was unsure and cautious. They were all so kind and loving, but I couldn't respond. I was not warmed by their love. As the first evening service began, I was really afraid that I had lost myself . . . and God. When our speaker for that service began to speak, things happened to me, for his words were: "God lives, God loves you. God wants you. Wherever you must go and whatever you must do, God has been there before you and now he walks with you." What a change came over me. The warmth of the Holy Spirit filled me as I had not known it for many months. Great hot sobs made their way out of my throat as I listened to this man tell of the love that God had for me. I felt that now I could live again! Now I could hear God calling to me and feel the love of the Saints.

The speaker said that he had changed his sermon after he was in the pulpit, for he sensed the loneliness among the members of the congregation. I was not the only one suffering from loneliness, but I know that God was speaking to me through this message for I seemed to be the only person there.

My husband received his ordination to the office of elder

and we returned to Italy filled with the prospects of work to be done. When I conduct a women's meeting, or sing in the choir, or am in some situation which enables me to tell of the love I have for God, or to witness for my church, I have the assurance that God has been here before me and now stands beside me.

Months have rolled by since the retreat in Germany and I miss the fellowship of my brethren, but I am still warmed by their love, their kindness, their testimonies, and their prayers. With them, all over Europe, they carry this love. Whether they are in isolated situations like mine or in church groups, they are working and striving to do the will of their Father in heaven who loves them.

As for me . . . the *church* is not here, but *God* is. I am here: I will serve Him.

The Living God Speaks Today

By Alan Tyree

We believe in divine revelation. Of major importance to an understanding of the movement, its beliefs, and its history is an understanding of the way in which revelatory experience has guided and continues to lead the church. Accessibility to God and dependence upon him for spiritual and contemporary direction are aspects of the essential foundation of the faith of the Saints. We believe that God desires to disclose himself and his will to all men, in all ages, everywhere.

There are, however, various concepts as to how this loving Father expresses himself. Much of this variety may relate to human differences, for it is always to man and through man that God speaks. As the Infinite attempts to communicate with the finite mind, He finds it necessary to speak in terms that are understood by man. Illustrative of this aspect of revelation is the following account from the church's mission in French Polynesia.

Early in 1969 an accident occurred at the church in Papeete, Tahiti, which brings into focus the love of God for his children as he seeks to reveal himself to his servants. The story focuses on Elder Taiura Piehi who died of injuries sustained when part of the ceiling of the Tarona Church collapsed during a study class at a mission conference. Here is how it happened.

Taiura was one of a group of extraordinary men who are God's men. He was always ready to serve the Lord and his church, and freely devoted himself and all he possessed in consecrated service. Because he made himself available, he was often asked to accept assignments for ministry in the outer island congregations of the mission. He was a carpenter, and frequently served as a builder of churches while offering spiritual ministry on weekends and evenings. His handiwork may be seen in both buildings and men.

On Thursday evening, January 16, 1969, he was lying on the living room couch after supper. Suddenly he arose and said to his wife and others of the home, "A Spirit has come to tell me that my work is finished. I know that I am going to die. Here is how it will happen: Your eyes will not see it, but someone else will come and tell you—that's how you will learn of it." Although his family tried to dissuade him from such notions, attributing them to a bad dream, he was insistent in his conviction that God had spoken to him in this way. He said to his wife, "When I die, you must remain steadfast in the church; for there is where we covenanted to serve from our marriage until this very day. I am telling you the truth. A messenger has just come to me and told me that my work is finished, and I shall die. . . ."

The next day he set about making preparations for his anticipated departure. He bought paint and spent most of the day painting the interior of his house. He knew that he would not be able to do it later. That evening, with fellow ministers of the neighborhood, he discussed the joys he had found in ministry—the missionary journeys he had made, the people he had baptized, the men he had called and ordained, the churches he had built, the hopes he had for loved ones in their services for Christ.

The following morning, Saturday, the mission conference and the scheduled classes began. He went to the Tarona Church in Papeete for the conference, while his wife, who was not feeling well, stayed home. It was that morning that the accident occurred. Seriously injured and unconscious he was rushed to the hospital while a young man ran to tell Sister Piehi.

During the days following the accident and prior to his death, he was a minister to all who knew and loved him. He was concerned for others who might have been injured, and rejoiced that he had borne the brunt of the accident. His wife, in an interview for *Te Orometua,* a Tahitian language publication for the mission in French Polynesia, recorded:

"He spoke to us, telling us to be courageous, that he would not get well, that he would die as a result of his injuries. He also said to me that we should not carry any doubts in our minds concerning his death resulting from the collapse of the ceiling; that he had reached the end of his work. He also said to his brother and sister that they should not be upset because of the accident, but that this was an indication to his relatives of the nature of his life's work, and of the depth of his standing in the

17

church, that he should die there. But it was not as a result of the ceiling; rather his work was done, and the Spirit of God had told him that his work was finished."

He reminded them of his oft-given counsel to them and said: "If you love me, follow the path I have followed."

Very early on Wednesday morning, just prior to his passing, one of his closest friends came in order to be with him and his near relatives. His wife described what happened in these words:

"As we stood beside his bed, he said to Nui [Elder Nui Arahu], 'Don't you see who is at the door? Stand aside.' And we looked with dread, because we saw no one. Then he said, 'You cannot see but I can see a person bearing a chair and he indicates that this is to be the nature of my dwelling place. It is a very beautiful chair that has been prepared for me, and it is covered with embroidery and crowned with stars. So while you shall remain, I want to ascend to this dwelling place....' "

Shortly after this, he died.

From this remarkable experience, several principles about divine revelation may be observed. First of all, *man brings to the revelatory experience all of his background, including those understandings (whether correct or not) that are rooted in his past experiences.* It is of interest to note the origin of Brother Piehi's vision of his "dwelling place" being a chair. In the Tahitian Bible, the fourteenth chapter of John reads like this: "In my Father's house are many *parahiraa;* if it were not so, I would have told you. I go to prepare a place for you." The term *parahiraa* contains a rather extended meaning. It means a place where one sits, or dwells, or abides. It can refer to a geographic area such as a village, city, island, homeland, etc. It can also mean one's domicile, residence, or house. But it can also mean anything upon which a person may be seated—a bench, a pew, a sofa, or a chair. In place of the English word "mansions," the translators correctly rendered the passage in Tahitian by the word "parahiraa"; however, in Taiura's mind this apparently meant a specific chair or seat which an angel of the Lord could carry with him as he appeared to Taiura. If the Lord had wished to convey the same message to one who was more conversant with the translation of the King James Bible, the vision would have taken on different aspects. Most likely a mansion house rather than a chair would have been associated with the angel in the vision.

Second, in the revelatory experience, *God meets man at the level where he is, within the framework of his limitations.* In order to say to Taiura that which he wished to communicate, God did not choose to lift him out of the context of his total life's experience. He did not choose to implant some totally new understandings, nor to burst in upon Taiura's consciousness with some unexpected and perhaps even previously misunderstood concepts or body of information. God did not choose to reveal to Taiura the nature of that "dwelling place" which he has prepared for him—nor ought it be supposed that the English word *mansions* is any better than the Tahitian word *parahiraa* in describing what the realms of eternity are really like. Notions about these things are quite insignificant in comparison with what God wanted to say to Taiura at that time. It pleased God to meet Taiura where he was, at his level of understanding.

Third, the revelatory experience *communicates the will of God for man in a given context, and does not necessarily state precise propositions for any and all unknown contexts and situations.* Man would be untrue to God and to the revelatory experience if he were to assume that Christ literally has a chair for each one in his "Father's house." God was attempting to offer ministry which was needed at a given time and in a given place. He had something which he wanted urgently to say to Taiura, and it really didn't have very much to do with what his dwelling place in the hereafter would look like. The message to be given and the ministry to be offered by God were of significantly greater consequence than to reveal the nature of a specific chair. God only used the context of Taiura's life, Taiura's mind, and Taiura's understanding in order to be able to minister to a dying man, his relatives, his many friends, and even to many whom Taiura did not know, because of their particular needs at that and a subsequent time. It was to a particular situation that God spoke, and any enduring and universal principle which may be drawn from the experience must take into consideration the entire context into which God spoke.

Fourth, *the purpose of the revelatory experience is to minister to man, and through him to others.* For such an accident to happen to one of the finest of God's servants, and in a building which had been dedicated to God, would represent a sore trial to anyone's faith. The average person cannot help but ask how God could let such a thing happen. Ministry was needed to prevent such an occurrence from becoming a severe stumbling block to the faith of relatives, friends, and members of the church. Indeed, some nonmembers did ask Sister Piehi after the accident how she could possibly refrain from anger toward the church and disbelief in its teachings. But out of the total experience of being forewarned and prepared for the catastrophe, ministry was given by Taiura to his loved ones and to the church as a whole. Furthermore, many whom Taiura never knew were blessed by his testimony and the testimony of his wife. Due to the unusual nature of his dying, and at the final moments when the faith of his loved ones would be tried, God offered revelatory ministry to his servant—and through him to others.

Finally, through the revelatory experience, *man finds an expression of the incarnation, a revelation of the Christ.* It is the Christ himself who is revealed, and not some intermediate body of knowledge that could obscure the revelation of the nature of God. Out of Taiura's experience, something is learned about the compassion of a loving Father, and discovery is made about how he discloses himself through human events, in spite of man's limitations and frailties. In much the same way that Jesus could say that the blind man's illness was for the purpose "that the works of God should be made manifest" (John 9:3), and that Lazarus' death was "for the glory of God, that the Son of God might be glorified thereby . . . to the intent that ye may believe" (John 11:4, 15), it may be said that through Taiura's experience it is the Christ who is revealed in his power and loving-kindness.

To the degree that any man has ever received a disclosure of God's will and purpose in him, that man not only heard a call and received a commission to act but also found himself possessed by God. The apostle Paul said, "Christ liveth in me," and John rightly said (as a part of the revelatory experience which God shared with him), "The testimony of Jesus is the spirit of prophecy" (Revelation 19:10). The very nature and spirit of prophecy or revelation is that the life of Jesus might be seen in the lives of men as a particular testimony of him. Words alone do not testify perfectly of anyone or anything. As symbols, words are valuable and helpful, but they remain only symbols standing for something more real and tangible. The *word* needs to be incarnate, to be lived out in human life, if it is to be fully clothed with meaning. "The word became flesh and dwelt among us"—this is a fact of history. But it is also true that God intends that his *word* is to become flesh.

Taiura's life, taken as a whole, testifies of the Lord whom

he served and whose attributes he determined to emulate in his own life. But it is also out of this unique experience with Deity that Taiura testifies to others, not about chairs and falling ceilings but about an all-encompassing particularizing love that is concerned for each individual as an individual and a tender mercy which reaches into distressed lives and brings peace, hope, and faith.

This is to bear witness that God continues to speak to all who will listen to him and heed his *word* through obedience, thus making a reality of that revelation by the principle of incarnation. God lives and speaks today. He desires to speak to all men and to live in them.

Out of Darkness, Light

By Vivian Losh North

I was one of those fortunate people brought up in a Christian home. Through crisis after crisis in our home, my mother's undying faith stood as the greatest testimony in my life. I have known my Lord since I was a youngster. I have felt his presence everywhere. And I have been given strength many times in difficult situations by his grace. Although I was nurtured on the fruits of Methodism, I took it for granted that it was not the one true church—and it never claimed to be.

The new opportunities I received after graduation from high school allowed me to embark on the greatest adventure of my life—that of finding Christ's true church. Soon after enrolling in Colorado State College, Greeley, Colorado, I set out to explore the religious world. By the process of elimination among those denominations with which I was acquainted, I chose the Christian Church. I was very much impressed with their doctrine of baptism by immersion; but, consequently, I was surprised and disappointed when they accepted my sprinkling baptism as valid. They made me feel very welcome but that certain "intangible" was lacking.

One afternoon a newly acquired friend invited me to attend a "missionary meeting" to be held at the Utah Mormon church that very evening. I was instantly interested and readily agreed to accompany her. Two young missionaries very zealously mapped out the plan of salvation. As they explained, the webs and tangles unraveled to form a perfect picture. I knew it was true. There was not one doubt. I felt akin to the blind man whose darkness fell as the scales from his eyes. I could indeed say that it was the most beautiful horizon in my life. I read. I studied. I rejoiced. I was even given a testimony of the truthfulness of the Book of Mormon.

Overwhelmed with a desire to spread this "good news," I decided to tell everyone I knew, and—if afforded the opportunity—those I didn't know. Among my friends I met with everything from indifference to the "it will wear off" attitude. However, when I told my sister I was planning to be baptized immediately, she became openly upset. She convinced me I should talk to her Lutheran pastor. He brought with him a chart with which he illustrated some strange doctrines taught by the Mormon church. In addition to the doctrines of polygamy and celestial marriage, there were two doctrines listed which were most repugnant to me. The first one was the Adam-God belief. The pastor quoted from Brigham Young: "He [Adam] is our father and our God, and the only God with whom we have to do." And of the Son of God another strange doctrine: "The Father has begotten him

[Jesus Christ] in His own likeness, He was not begotten of the Holy Ghost. And who is the Father? He is the first of the Human family."

I was shocked and bitterly disillusioned. The missionaries had told me the truth and I had accepted it as such. Unfortunately, what they had left unsaid could not be reconciled with the God I knew existed. I rejected any further association with them.

Later, in 1961, I moved to Moorhead, Iowa. One evening shortly after, I was introduced to a young man from that city who had just returned from an RLDS youth meeting. I interrogated him concerning the Reorganized group: Did he believe in polygamy or celestial marriage? Did he believe in an "Adam-God" theory? . . . etc. His answers, of course, were no. He continued to explain that the Reorganized Church was the lawful continuation of the original church and that the present president and prophet was the grandson of the prophet Joseph Smith. He assured me that the church opposed these doctrines which I had mentioned. Having received these satisfactory answers, I was convinced that this was the Lord's church.

Past experiences had taught me caution so I spent one year of study. Then I was baptized and confirmed into the Reorganized Church of Jesus Christ of Latter Day Saints. I shall always cherish those moments, as I will cherish every moment of my unforgettable adventure. I eagerly anticipate the future because I am convinced that as long as I remain converted to the gospel of Jesus Christ there will always be mountains to climb, obstacles to overcome, challenges to be met, worlds to be won for Christ. Indeed, what greater adventures than these?

God Does Not Change

By Cecil Ettinger

Just before leaving the bush country of Nigeria in 1963, I came out of a jungle hut one morning and noticed some rather intricate markings upon the ground. I was told that these indicated the worship of JuJu, the ancient pagan tribal religion. The night before, semi-nude people gathered around a flickering fire and paid homage to the god of the tree, the god of the river, the god of the light, and the god of the darkness. Later that day, I met with about 250 people in a small, rudely built chapel. They sang hymns to the rhythmic beat of the drums, danced single file to the altar to make their offerings, and spoke of the one God of heaven and earth and his Only Begotten Son, Jesus Christ. Less than two weeks later, I met with other brethren in a rather sophisticated service of worship in England. Included in the service of worship was a beautifully executed musical number, a thought-provoking responsive reading, and a logical, well thought out sermon concerning the unchangeability of God.

These three separate and yet connected experiences provoke several questions. Were these three services of worship directed toward the same God? Does God change in order to meet individual needs and situations? Do people seek God out of their own situations and come to understand him according to the limits of their experience and intellect?

Recently I was talking to a young person who was sincerely searching for a knowledge of God, yet in his searching cried out in despair, "I have never had any religious or mystical experiences. When I try to pray, my prayers go no higher than the ceiling. It seems as if I am just talking to myself." He was on the verge of giving up the quest—yet all the time God was there. He was expecting to be bowled over by some great emotional experience. Finally, during our conversation, he recognized that it was God who had prompted him to look for Him in the first place. Pascal was truly inspired of the Holy Spirit when he made the Lord say, "Comfort yourself; you would not seek me if you had not found me." God is the initiator as well as the result of our quest to know him.

This raises two important questions. Can we know something without knowing that we know it? And can knowledge be all around us without ever being perceived? Let us answer the second question first. A couple of years ago I went to the Biltmore Mansion in Ashville, North Carolina. It is a beautiful mansion which now serves as a tourist attraction. We were ushered into the library and told that it contained 10,000 volumes, carefully selected to represent the greatest writings of our world. I was startled to find, however, that no one ever touched these volumes except the cleaning woman who occasionally dusted them. Here was the distilled knowledge of the ages all around us, yet none of us could perceive that knowledge unless we could take the time to open the books, peruse them, and make their information our own. Think what Lincoln did with one book, a shovel, and the light of the fireplace. Yes, knowledge can be all around us and we may never perceive it unless we earnestly seek to understand.

And now the first question. Can I know something without knowing that I know it? Most of us have had the experience of looking back and seeing the real meaning of something long after it has happened. In 1944, a plane I was flying was hit by enemy aircraft fire. The airplane limped and struggled. I pushed and pulled everything in the cockpit, and finally I landed in a wooded area just behind friendly lines.

On another occasion, while dive bombing an ammunition dump, I made a direct hit. The dump exploded and violently threw my aircraft high into the air, but I flew the undamaged aircraft back to the base without incident. These experiences seemed quite ordinary at the time. Weeks later, however, the true significance of what had happened began to weigh heavily upon me. I can truly say that much of my life has been shaped by the sensing of what I knew at that moment but did not know that I knew. What most of us need today is not new knowledge or experience but the ability to understand the knowledge and experience which we already have. Jacob at Bethel said, "Surely the Lord was in this place and I knew it not." Most of the great church leaders of former days did not have experiences remarkably different from our own. They did possess the spiritual perceptivity to understand what was happening and the spiritual skill to interpret so that it could be of benefit to others.

"He comprehendeth all things, and all things are before him, and all things are round about him; and he is above all things, and in all things, and is through all things, and is round about all things: and all things are by him, and of him; even God, for ever and ever."— Doctrine and Covenants 85:10c.

Belief in God is basic and of the greatest importance. Whether we are ignorant savages around the campfire, persons groping for the truth in simple worship service, or cosmopolitan members of advanced society, the evidence of God is all about us. By listening to those who have known God, by being unbiased in our own search for him, and by letting him evidence himself to us in his way rather than demanding the evidence by our own pattern, we can come to know him.

We believe that God is the ultimate, supreme, unchangeable, infinite, creative Person of the universe. Probably the greatest evidence of an unchanging God is his unchanging personality. Wherever we see law, order, beauty, and purpose, we see an example of personality. If I walk down the street and find tiny metal fragments, I might assume they had come there by chance. However, if I see wheels and gears and springs fit carefully together into a functioning watch, I rightly conclude that a personality has put these together for a particular purpose. The universe shows greater grandeur, more intricate systems and orderly arrangement—perfect timing to the ultimate degree. Such organization and purposeful order give evidence of a supreme Person.

If I walk down this same street and see two houses side by side, I can tell a lot about the builder by the nature of the building. The first may have wood as a foundation, topped by layers of brick, and finally stone. I conclude that the builder changed his mind as he built, thinking first that wood was the better building material, deciding that brick was better, and finally concluding that stone was what he wanted. In contrast, the other house may show orderly arrangement with stone as the foundation—the entire structure beautifully fit together and conclusively directed. I conclude that this builder had a plan from the beginning and that he was unchanging in his design.

The universe offers evidence again of the unchanging, eternal nature of the stars in the heaven, of the earth on which we live, of the molecules and atoms which are the building blocks of the universe. The unchangeable nature of the most intricate of these building blocks bears evidence of an unchanging God.

"When I consider thy heavens, the work of thy fingers, the moon and the stars, which thou hast ordained; what is man, that thou art mindful of him? and the son of man, that thou visitest him? For thou hast made him a little lower than the angels, and hast crowned him with glory and honor."—Psalm 8:3-5.

"For the natural man is an enemy to God, and has been, from the fall of Adam, and will be, for ever and ever; but . . . he yields to the enticings of the Holy Spirit, and putteth off the natural man, and becometh a saint, through the atonement of Christ, the Lord, and becometh as a child, submissive, meek, humble, patient, full of love, willing to submit to all things which the Lord seeth fit to inflict upon him, even as a child doth submit to his father."—Mosiah 1:119, 120.

Man is a curious paradox. At his best he is a little lower than the angels, willing to sacrifice his own life for an ideal, his religion, or the life of a friend. He is generous, benevolent, concerned, and unselfish. At his worst, man shames the animals. He is greedy, lustful, cruel. During World War II, I was assigned on one occasion to ride the lead tank of an armored column in order to direct air-to-ground activities with the squadron to which I was assigned. On several occasions during this particular tour of duty, we were engaged in the heated pitch of that battle. I have seen men in that situation kill with a vengeance, literally ripping apart their foes. In the lull of battle, however, I saw one man tenderly pick up a frozen bird from the snow and place it under his tunic to try to revive it.

What causes this dualistic nature of man? Every man, woman, and child in the world, provided he has his full faculty of mind, possesses within him certain intimations of the presence of God. If one fights these intimations and allows selfishness and greed to predominate, he will gravitate in one direction. On the other hand, if he seeks to know God and truly finds him, the qualities of unselfishness and love will abound. This is true in the underdeveloped areas of the world as well as in the highest peaks of civilization. My first illustration of the three worship services did not so much indicate the changing nature of God because of the way people sought him as the changing nature of men as they try to comprehend an eternal, unchangeable God who is the source of all truth, beauty, and goodness.

Many people, however, look upon God as a mere illusion. Some have said that he is a crutch upon which man leans when he cannot depend upon himself. Others have labeled God as father-complex or wish-fulfillment. Still others have said that he does not exist in any way, that man's search for God merely shows his own lack of maturity. Some say that people who look to God are victims of illusion. They say he is a ghost. It is a basic truth, however, that the superstitious and unenlightened see something that is real and imagine it to be a phantom. The native in the forest sees the outline of a real tree and imagines it to be a spirit. The superstitious see a cloth fluttering in the wind and imagine it to be a ghost. On the other hand, the superstitious do not see spirits and imagine them to be real. So it is with the changeable nature of man in understanding God. The truly superstitious are those who have experience with the real God and imagine that experience to be false.

I once heard a sermon in which an apostle spoke of the major attributes of God as being truth, beauty, and goodness. This indicates something of the nature of God's eternal, unchangeable person, and man's changeable, progressive person as he strives toward God.

God is truth. Everyone knows the pressure of truth upon an individual's life. I have known individuals who have made the practice of lying so much a part of their lives that the time has come when they preferred telling a lie to telling the truth. However, this type of individual usually admits that there was a time in his life when he was more comfortable when he told the truth. Psychologists might say that the reason for this is that society conditions him to tell the truth. But why should society condition him? Philosophers will ultimately admit that truth is an attribute of reality or, as I prefer to say, an attribute of God. It therefore follows that man's desire for truth is a desire for God.

God is beauty. Man also has a need to create that which is beautiful and disregard that which is ugly. Again, man's nature can be perverted and this desire for beauty can be lost through wickedness or conditioning. This is also true of a person's standards for what is beautiful and what is ugly. These standards may change from time to time or from culture to culture. Man nevertheless strives for that which he considers beautiful. His striving for beauty is actually a striving for God.

God is goodness. As previously stated, standards of right and wrong vary from age to age and culture to culture. It is also true, however, that no matter what the society or the age, certain standards of right and wrong, of goodness and badness are established. In very primitive societies this standard of goodness might be that which is best for a very privileged few. As civilization advances, and as people are truly concerned with God, their standard of goodness is that which is best for the most people with regard for personality and the value of the individual. We would conclude, therefore, that wherever there is ultimate truth or beauty or goodness it comes from God; God puts the desire for truth, beauty, and goodness in our minds and hearts. He also gives us the capacity to appreciate them.

John stated in his first epistle, "Yes, we love him because he first loved us." Religion is man's search for God because He has first sought us. God is unchangeable since he has striven from age to age to bring man unto himself. His very unchangeable nature is the source of all truth, beauty, and goodness. He strives to help us comprehend his eternal nature so that we may be companions to him. Man changes in both his capacity and his willingness to understand. Our capacity is greater in this age because we can build upon the unselfish lives of all those who have preceded us in the search to understand God. Our willingness is conditioned by the degree that we recognize the ultimate Source of life and strive to understand Him.

A Step in Faith

By Peter Wells

My first contact with the church came while playing in a table tennis tournament sponsored by the Methodist Church. Two sisters (members of the RLDS Church who were playing in the tournament) attracted my attention and I asked one to meet me the following evening. Her reply was encouraging and although she declined an invitation to my church I arranged a meeting outside her church after the Sunday evening service. To avoid the possibility of not finding it I drove around the part of town in which it was located during the afternoon. I was not impressed by the building's appearance—or the name. My adverse impressions seemed to be confirmed a few minutes later when I read in a book that Joseph Smith claimed revelations from God and had written the Book of Mormon. The book also stated that he had been a polygamist. My fears were alleviated by the warm reception and genuine interest that were expressed by just about every member of the Sutton-in-Ashfield Branch when I went to meet her.

As far as my church affiliation was concerned I had been christened into the Church of England. Around the age of fourteen I had entered into junior membership in the Methodist Church and later, following a family tradition, I became a full member. I also started to train for local preaching.

Perhaps I should reflect somewhat upon an earlier period before I continue with what happened after my experience at the church. Just prior to and during the early part of my service with the Royal Air Force I drifted away from church and Christianity. I became convinced that the way of life I was then leading was mature, that the steps I had taken were intellectually honest, and that I had found freedom from the inhibiting factors of previous generations. Despite this conviction I was not truly happy or satisfied, for life had little real purpose. I would examine each of my goals and aims and ask the question, "Then what?" and in the final answer could find no satisfaction in the purposeless finitude of life.

I can still vividly remember the black despair which caused me to cry out to a God who did not answer and the feeling of hopelessness that prevented healthy sleep for periods of months.

In the period prior to induction I had studied for a career in company management. I had worked in this field before my conscription into the forces. During the time before and after conscription I continued my search for purpose and meaning to my life. I read extensively in mythology, Eastern religions, psychology, philosophy, and spent a lot of time asking searching questions of all who believed that life had some purpose.

During this period I gradually found my childhood values eroding. I would argue vehemently what the world should do or the way the other people should live their lives. On subjects such as the inability of the Christian gospel to meet

33

man's needs, capital punishment, war, freedom, racism, discipline, atomic catastrophes, voting at eighteen, sexual permissiveness, censorship, capitalism, and colonialism I could hold forth with voracity and lucidity. Yet my own way of *living* and the things I actually *did* were in many ways a contradiction of my arguments.

This was not disturbing, however, for (with logic sublime in its ignorance) I excused myself by using four traditional arguments:

1. I'm being moderate in all things.
2. I'm allowed a few lapses due to my preferred status (It applies to others but not to me).
3. I'm not harming anyone.
4. I would try harder if everyone else did.

It was much later that I discovered these arguments all contain the same essential element of deceit. They allowed me to absolve myself from personal responsibility for my pattern of life. They did not commit me to an affirmative decision to change my way of life, nor did they set up an objective standard upon which my life could be measured. These were arguments for maintaining the status quo, but as I have said, I was frustrated and unhappy. I felt that I was at a crossroads in my life and that ineluctably I was having decisions made for me which were leading me where I didn't really want to go.

During this crucial period I was serving in Aden, at the southern end of the Red Sea. I returned to my camp one evening to find a new room-mate who had arrived from England only that day. When I first saw him he was on his knees praying. We became firm friends and although his Roman Catholicism did not attract me, I soon found myself praying again and I became involved in the mixed Protestant church on camp. Given the association of other young men whose efforts were directed to living better lives, mine also improved, and just prior to flying back home for "demob" I thought I would prepare to fulfill a lifelong desire—that of becoming a minister in the Methodist Church. Somehow, despite the vicissitudes of life, I had always known I would serve as a minister in a full-time capacity. This unexplained belief never left me, even when I was baptized in the church just twelve months after the table tennis tournament which introduced me to my wife and the church.

My business career prospered and my wife and I were happy to worship in the Sutton-in-Ashfield Branch. It was here in legendary Robin Hood country that I was first called to the priesthood and received some fine experiences in the fellowship of the Saints. During the spring and summer of 1967 it seemed that God brought us to another crucial point of decision. My wife and I inexplicably knew that we would soon be asked to serve our Lord full time. One evening the presiding church officer of Britain phoned and told us that he and Apostle Aleah Koury wanted to meet us. Our faith in the revelation of church appointment was confirmed when we were sent to Independence, Missouri, on our first church assignment exactly five years after my having been baptized.

During the week that we made our decision to accept full-time appointment I had an offer for a job I had been working toward for years. It would have given us just about everything life could offer—but it would have taken us to Ireland and away from the church. Imagine our surprise when we discovered that six other full-time ministers who were appointed about the same time had had similar offers the very week of their decision. I believe that the pattern of my life was guided by God and that he led me to membership and service in this church. If the period of despair in my life taught me anything it was that the way back to hope is not the easy way of escape. Prayers, if they are to be answered, have to be prayed, and a positive, optimistic application of gospel principles will bring maturing experiences.

I cannot point to any one thing and say that it is the reason for my believing that this church is specially and divinely commissioned. I believe this church has been called into being by God. He has restored to the earth those factors which are necessary for man to comprehend the fullness of the gospel of Jesus Christ—the gospel of the light and life of men. I have had many experiences since coming into the church for which there is no atheistically logical answer. These experiences confirm my testimony, but do not in any way form the basis of it. The basis of my belief in the divinity of this church stems from my belief in a creator God who is able to communicate and express his power to man in an unmistakable and meaningful manner.

As I respond in a positive way to the deepest yearnings and desires of my innermost self, the power of God becomes observable and knowable to me. I find it impossible to live a life without faith or propositions. I lived the proposition "There is no God" and found frustration, despair, and hopelessness as my bedfellows. I am living the proposition "God is" and have found purpose, hope, and satisfaction. For example, let me say it this way. I know my wife loves me not because of the things she does or says but because of a trust—a faith—I have in her. The things that she does and says confirm but do not form the basis of my belief in her love. The basis is faith and trust. Similarly God confirms in a powerful way my step of faith—my trust or proposition in him. As I worship, as I pray, or as I exercise even a small particle of faith I become increasingly confident in the rightness of my trust.

As I went into the waters of baptism at the age of twenty-three I was aware that this was a step in faith. From that time God through his Son has confirmed the rightness of that act in many ways. I have become increasingly aware that I was not joining a church in the commonly accepted sense of the word but that I was exercising my agency in accepting the challenge offered by Jesus in the twenty-eighth chapter of Matthew where it is written:

"Go ye therefore, and teach all nations, baptizing them in the name of the Father, and of the Son, and of the Holy Ghost: teaching them to observe all things whatsoever I have commanded you: and, lo, I am with you alway, even unto the end of the world. Amen."

I am certain that many men are responding to the Holy Spirit as God seeks to establish his purposes in their hearts. I am also certain that Jesus Christ is personally working with this people that we may be perfect mediators of his gospel in its completeness. People are prompted by God to respond to physical human needs and their work is essential and commendable. He has given the members of the church another role. I see this as motivating others, mediating God's love to them through sharing the fuller life and granting a vision of the future kingdom which has developed through the added knowledge found in the Book of Mormon and the revelations of Latter Day Saint prophets.

Through this knowledge we are able to demonstrate that the sacraments and ordinances of the church are more than just symbolical scenes of divine drama; they carry inherent power for those who participate willingly, humbly, expectantly, and wisely.

For Reorganized Latter Day Saints the sacraments and ordinances, while containing symbolical elements, are more than mere symbols. This can be seen easily from the adverse effects on the lives of those who cease to participate in the sacraments or, conversely, the effects on the lives of those who commence to participate in the manner described above. Many psychologists feel that the sacraments and ordinances fill a deep need which contributes to the physical, mental, and spiritual well-being of the individual, thus emphasizing the powerful therapeutic value of participation.

All of us are free agents. We are free to worship, witness, and work for Him who gave us life, purpose, hope, and fulfillment. After years of searching I have found in this church the clearest and finest expression of God's purpose for his creation.

I now have a purpose to which I can align my work and life. Hope burns brightly, for I can actually see God's purpose being fulfilled in my friends, the church, my work, and in me. Zion is no longer an ideal so far away that the distance detracts from its viability. Just as early Christians called Jesus *Emmanuel,* "God with us," so I can say *Zion* which means to me, "God's purposes are here." I have hope and optimism that in this church I can make a distinctive contribution in the process of defeating the forces of evil, mediating the Redeemer of society, and establishing the kingdom of God here on this earth.

These Are My Friends

By Robert G. Fisher

Let me tell you of three people who mean a lot to me and who have taught me about some of the fundamentals of my religion. Two are convicts in the Maryland Penitentiary. The third is a convict's wife. I became associated with them when the warden asked me to meet with eleven convicts who are seeking to start a Maryland chapter of the Seven Steps Foundation, a convict self-help organization bearing some similarity to Alcoholics Anonymous.

Chris is thirty-nine. He is intelligent and articulate. He has a straightforward approach in conversation and a pleasant, courteous manner. He has considerable organizational ability. He once managed to arrange (in part by drawing his own legal papers) to have himself, a confederate, and a pistol arrive simultaneously in the back seat of a police car on the way to a court appearance and so escaped from prison briefly. Chris is something of an "operator" in the state-use printing shop, and without title or official authority handles responsibilities equaling those of foreman. He approaches his work with great care although he earns less than a dollar a day for his efforts. At sixteen he was the leader of a Boy Scout troop, having taken over when the troop's regular Scoutmaster was drafted into the Army. Chris nearly became an Eagle Scout, but instead ran away to join the Army himself. His life turned, he says, when he committed some minor offense and was sent to jail in Oregon. He remembers how frightened he was on his first night in jail and is convinced that if someone had tried to reach him then he would never have become a criminal. However, no one came that night.

Chris is now serving consecutive sentences in the Maryland Penitentiary for armed robbery and escape aggregating 122 years. When Maryland is finished with him, California wants him to do five sentences of five years to life. Then Arizona wants him.

Chris, who fought for his sanity during three years of solitary confinement after an escape attempt, is a determinedly realistic man. He knows the odds are slim that he will ever leave prison legitimately before he reaches old age. He also is coming to realize, although relatively recently, that the odds are even slimmer that he will stay for long on the outside if he escapes again. Four escapes followed by quick reincarceration have taught him that.

Chris is enthusiastic about the part of the Seven Steps program which will enable him to meet with juvenile delinquents and try to steer them away from the attitudes which led him to a life in prison. He is also a principal inmate organizer of the part of the program which is designed to help other, shorter-term inmates "make it" on the outside after they are paroled. However, true to his candid approach, Chris makes no pretensions to having suddenly become an altruist. His main ambition is directed at the slim chance that if he devotes himself to the constructive activities in the penitentiary, a miracle will happen that will somehow enable him to leave prison legitimately while still in the prime of life. He wants back the life he threw away. He is willing to work as long and as hard as most ambitious men work to achieve success just for the chance to start at the beginning again.

Gayanne is twenty-seven. She met Don, now forty-one, when he was on parole after serving fifteen years in the Texas Penitentiary. They were married after a short courtship. When it appeared that Gayanne might be pregnant, Don began to drink heavily. On the night that Gayanne's pregnancy was medically confirmed, Don was arrested for burglarizing the apartment above the store in which he worked. Don is now serving a ten-year sentence in Maryland. His Texas parole having been revoked, he owes Texas ten more years upon completion of his Maryland sentence. Gayanne and their two-year-old daughter live in Baltimore and visit Don in prison as often as permitted (once a week). Gayanne's parents have disinherited her and return her letters because she has insisted upon sticking by Don.

Her attitude toward Don's imprisonment seems quite

realistic. "When my daughter gets older," she says, "I will tell her that her father is in prison because he did something wrong and has to be punished." Then she adds, "However, when Don gets out I will tell her that he has been punished, and when punishment is over that's the end of the matter." Gayanne lives with the knowledge that Don has a drinking problem and that he probably committed the relatively stupid burglary of the apartment over his place of employment in response to a subconscious drive to escape the added responsibilities of parenthood. She knows that even if he is lucky enough to be paroled from both Maryland and Texas after five or six years more of imprisonment he will be in danger of succumbing to the same weaknesses again. However, she loves Don and wants to do everything possible to bring about the day when their daughter can live in a home with both of her parents. Gayanne has taken her marriage vows seriously.

Angelo is in his mid-forties. He has committed over one hundred robberies in his lifetime. He is now serving twenty years in Maryland for armed robbery. California has detainers on him for violating his parole there from sentences for armed robbery and first-degree murder. He knows that the odds that California will drop its detainers if he is paroled in Maryland are slim because he was previously paroled and returned as a parole violator on two occasions in California before getting the parole which led to his present Maryland incarceration. In short, he has already struck out three times.

As is the case with Chris, Angelo's intelligence and ability coupled with the daring nature of the crimes he committed have made him a penitentiary leader. However, unlike Chris, he does not entertain even a slim hope of leaving the penitentiary before old age. On several occasions I have heard Angelo explain his presence in the Seven Steps program as "I want to be a man." Translated that means, "I want to do something with the remainder of my life that will enable me to respect myself."

Angelo is an emotional man, which may or may not have something to do with his Greek ancestry and upbringing in southern Europe. I remember him best from the tears that were in his eyes the first time we saw each other after I wrote him a letter stating, among other things, that he and I should consider ourselves co-therapists during the Seven Steps meetings. The idea that I should consider him an equal partner in a ministry to others made Angelo—the murderer, robber, and high status "con"—cry. Sometimes I feel like crying myself when I consider the tragedy of this talented forty-five-year-old man facing the prospect of a lifetime alone in a foreign prison where he feels his existence is so little appreciated that a few words to the effect that he might have something to give bring tears to his eyes.

In the half year that I have known Chris, Angelo, Don, and Gayanne, they have become my friends as well as my partners in the Seven Steps venture. They are friends in every sense of the word—people I value for their virtues of honesty, loyalty, and courage as well as for their worthy aspirations. They are people I enjoy being with, people whose abilities I regard as complementary to my own, people I care about, people I trust to be loyal and considerate toward me. They have also been my teachers more profoundly than I have been theirs. They have taught me what Paul really meant when he wrote in I Corinthians 13 that hope, faith, and charity (i.e. caring) are greater spiritual gifts than prophecy, tongues, or miracles. Prophecy, tongues, and miracles are lesser gifts because their influence upon human beings is transitory; they excite for a time but rather quickly become mere memories or are forgotten. But hope, faith, and love are to the human spirit what electricity is to a light bulb—they illuminate and warm the soul and enable it to fulfill a purpose. Without hope, faith, or love, the human spirit soon finds itself imprisoned—in darkness, cold, unnoticed, having nothing to contribute, dead.

Editor's Note: Since the article originally appeared in the *Restoration Witness* several years ago it is a delight to record that Chris, Angelo, Don, and Gayanne are still progressing in their adjustments to society. Chris has developed a Jaycee Chapter in the Maryland Penitentiary that has taken national honors. He is also president of the Seven Steps program. Angelo is devoting his energies to positive, beneficial activities for himself and others. He is trying to live as a creative human being and productive social entity in spite of imprisonment. Gayanne is sticking by her husband, Don, who is still in the Maryland Penitentiary. Their daughter, Suzanne, is now about five years old. Don still has detainers against him in Texas and Florida, but there is hope that these detainers will be lifted in a year or two and Don will be able to progress to a minimum security situation in the Maryland Penitentiary. He would then become eligible for parole after six months or a year of satisfactory performance on work release.

Guided All the Way

By Roy H. Schaefer

"Having been born of goodly parents" is well-worn phraseology which nevertheless aptly describes my entrance into life. My parents, born in Germany, became associated with the "good news" of the Restoration movement through the miraculous intervention of the heavenly Father and a member of the church from Holland. Shortly thereafter they immigrated to the U.S.A. in hopes of making a contribution to the building up of the "New Jerusalem." Our home could best be described as centered in the words of the hymn written by President F. M. Smith, "Zion the beautiful beckons us on." When I was ten years old, we moved from New York City to Independence, Missouri. Here I enjoyed all the privileges of "growing up" in a community densely populated with church members.

As a senior in William Chrisman High School of Independence I participated in a special Vocational Day, and also took some vocational guidance tests. In addition to my own desires and interests these led me to focus my college studies in the direction of dentistry which became the major objective and goal of my life.

After two rewarding years at Graceland College and five years at the University of Missouri at Kansas City, I entered the United States Air Force. Several months prior to induction I made it a matter of prayer and fasting (especially seeking understanding and guidance) that wherever the Air Force might send me I would be granted opportunity to share in ministry. I was, to put it mildly, amazed to receive word that I was assigned to Alaska! A colleague, Dr. Howard Fultz, and I began frantically searching available resources about this land which at that time, 1957, was still a territory.

It was in Anchorage, Alaska, that I met with a nucleus of Saints, who, though they had some mannerisms and points of view different from my own, had one outstanding characteristic which left its mark indelibly upon my soul. They naturally and unselfishly shared a deep, rich, and sincere spirit of love for a somewhat lonely serviceman who was

44

away from his fiancée, friends, and home. Without question they took me into their homes, made me feel welcome, and, more importantly, accepted me as a part of their families. It was while I shared with these devoted people and the appointee, Seventy Eldon Dickens, that innumerable opportunities of ministry were opened to me.

After six months in Alaska, I returned to Independence and married. Marilyn returned with me to Alaska, and we were invited to serve as Zion's League leaders for a nucleus of nine Leaguers. Again, through their enthusiastic, inquisitive stimulation our lives were enriched. By sharing in a reunion on a tundra-covered island in beautiful Lake Louise, working in a mission in the farming community of Palmer, teaching the women's department class and preaching as a newly ordained teacher, I began coming to grips with some of the needs of mankind which can be met through the reconciliatory ministry of Jesus Christ.

As I neared the completion of my two-year tour with the U.S.A.F. I again felt the need to seek the guidance of the heavenly Father through prayer. When my wife and I took up residence in the community of our choice we wanted to be able to see and participate in areas of outreach and service. The next eight years saw this materialize far beyond our fondest hopes. Doors of opportunity which are available in the Center Place were opened. From a number of meaningful experiences and testimonies, I will share just one. I was asked by the stake president to serve as the presiding elder for a proposed new congregation in the Center Stake of Zion. When I discussed this possibility with my pastor, he shared the following piece of wise counsel: "If you want to grow, accept tasks bigger than you are." This guideline has been most helpful in my life.

An astronaut, Edward White II (who was the first American to walk in space and who met an untimely death through a malfunction of the dry-run Apollo mission on January 27, 1967), very adequately shared the following communication. He had received a letter, following his space walk, asking him about his beliefs. His reply in part was, ". . . as to the evidence of God's presence during our journey and that short period I walked in space, I did not feel any nearer to him there than here, but I do know his sure hand guided us *all the way*. . . ."

As I reflect upon my life, I would affirm with Astronaut White that God has graciously guided "all the way." It is almost a paradox that this fantastic age of great scientific and technological advancement is also an age of turmoil, agony, and crisis. I am becoming increasingly convinced that God through Jesus Christ is "the way" and that lasting joy shall come to man only as he finds meaningful, all-the-way relationships with Him.

My joy has been full in those moments when by his grace I have been permitted to see the creative capacities and potentialities fulfilled in numbers of people. I am moved when I read in *The Transparent Self,* by Dr. Sidney M. Jourard, "There is increasing scientific evidence that man's physical and psychological health are profoundly affected by the degree to which he has found meaning, direction, and purpose in his existence." Or to read from the works of Dr. Myron Allen in *Morphological Creativity* the suggestion that "The strongest motivation known to man is the desire to achieve his potentials, to be creative . . . and this lies inherent in each person." Or when I hear Dr. James Turpin, director of "Project Concern," in speaking of his work in Vietnam, Hong Kong, Mexico, and Tennessee say, "Happiness is as near as you can find one person to love." Or when I hear Evangelist Arthur Oakman say (and I paraphrase), "The only strengths we have that are worth dedicating are those we extend in behalf of another's weakness."

46

The church is *participation*. It is the privilege and responsibility of granting every person of every age, every social, economic, educational background and capacity who has committed himself to the cause of Christ, the opportunity to release, in loving service, the creative potentialities resident in his life. One of my deepest concerns is that there lies dormant in every congregation, branch, and mission tremendous untouched capabilities and resources of people.

Let me offer three guidelines which I follow:

(1) When invited to share in some role of church life, instead of saying "no," *try saying "yes."*

(2) If you are never asked to participate *offer your services* to those responsible.

(3) If you are still not asked, *go to work anyway* in some area of loving concern and meet some specific need of humanity in the community in which you live.

At a time when serious questions are being raised in respect to the role of the Christian church, its clergy and organizational structure, and when several denominational bodies are losing large numbers of members and are finding it increasingly difficult to raise finances, it may seem somewhat foolish or at least unwise to enlist in any religiously oriented endeavor. I reflect upon the vivid affirmation shared by God through the incarnational impact of his Son in an era of history which did not have peace and tranquillity. It was not a period when all problems were solved and "all was well." Rather, it was a period of confusion and crises yet it held opportunities for needed ministries.

I tend to agree with Dr. James S. Stewart of Edinburg who said: "The real problem of Christianity is not atheism or skepticism, but the non-witnessing Christian trying to smuggle his own soul into heaven."

Today, I sincerely hope that by his love I can match

myself to this hour of seemingly insurmountable social, economic, and theological considerations which have been unveiled in their stark reality to the world.

As He has been graciously, lovingly and, yes, often admonishingly with me, I want desperately to be with him "all the way."

Merry Christmas

By Maurice Draper

What more popular greeting on any special occasion is there than "Merry Christmas"? We do sometimes relate our greeting to the occasion on certain holidays, but how often does one hear, "Patriotic Independence Day!" or "Exciting Halloween!"? Occasionally we refer to the season when the special day is Thanksgiving, and we do so more frequently when we wish others a "Happy Easter!" But no other season grips our attention like Christmas does.

Our criticism of the commercialization of Christmas may be actually a recognition of its widespread impact. It isn't necessary to approve the commercial distortion of the meaning of Christmas to take note of the fact that many non-Christians everywhere are involved deeply in activities which originated in some way in the religious celebration of the birth of Jesus.

So for many reasons millions upon millions of people greet each other during this season with "Merry Christmas!" If many use the term casually and yet share to some degree in the spirit of the occasion, it surely behooves those of us who take the Christmas celebration most seriously to reflect upon its essential meaning.

That it is ambiguous (even to the serious-minded religious celebrant) is illustrated by the frequency with which an old English carol is misunderstood. How many of us sing lustily, "God rest you, merry gentlemen" when we ought to be singing, "God rest you merry, gentlemen"? Notice the different position of the comma. The word "merry" is not an adjective modifying "gentlemen." It is an adverb modifying "rest." The intent is a prayer, the essence of which is emphasized if we simply make it read "God rest you merry!"

What does this usage of "merry" mean? It is an obsolete word in this sense meaning "to cause happiness." Such modern definitions as frolicsome, mirthful, and hilarious are related to the old term, of course, but they are shallow and trivial compared with the meaning implied in the original phrasing of the carol.

"God rest you *merry!*" This reminds us of the Book of Mormon declaration, "Men are that they might have joy" (II Nephi 1:115). Both statements are related to the testimony of Jesus, "I am come that they might have life, and that they might have it more abundantly" and to his prayer "that they might have my joy fulfilled in themselves" (John 10:10, 17:13).

Such happiness as may be caused by the blessing of God is certainly more than trivial festiveness or hilarity. It is not merely the mirthfulness of a party but the solid, delightful satisfaction of creative living in good fellowship. A way of life is implied in the carol's frequently misunderstood line. Out of the way of life are derived pleasant satisfactions which were appropriately described by the archaic Middle English word "merry." So we really sing, "May God's way of life for man produce in you, gentlemen, a pleasant and delightful happiness."

Thus we see that the greeting "Merry Christmas" is itself a form of prayer. Every person who uses the term is voicing a petition that the meaning of Jesus' birth shall be realized in the life of the hearer. Perhaps the greeter is rarely aware of the fact that he is verbalizing a Christian prayer. But its inherent spirit makes it popular and the mood which accompanies the utterance is an expression of that spirit.

God works among us in many ways. It may be that even in the thoughtless repetition of the Christmas prayer-greeting both professing Christians and those who profess no religious commitments at all are reminded of the good spirit in which all men should live together.

Zion

By John W. Blackstock

As a young man I began to give serious consideration to my life and its proper relationship to the forces of the Almighty. I became intrigued with the idea of Zion as I then understood it to be taught by the church. I understood it to mean, then and now, a premillennial kingdom. It was for me the most challenging single item of theology which is propounded by the RLDS Church. I'm certain that through the years my concept of Zion has changed—I suspect this would be normal for anyone. But there have been certain basic concepts which have remained with me through these many years.

Frequently when one discusses the subject of Zion, he finds those who want to be technical in the phraseological use and meaning of some words. There are those who say that Zion is a stepping-stone to the kingdom of God. There are others who think of Zion and the kingdom as being synonymous. For the purpose of this testimony, may we assume that Zion and the kingdom of God are synonymous, that Zion in its state of perfection (or near perfection) prior to the coming of the millennium would be an expression of the kingdom of God. Let us admit in the beginning that the kingdom of God will never find its full perfection or its finest expression until He, whose right it is to reign, shall come again and reign among his people in the millennium. May we assume that the early elders of the church were right when many of them contended that the purpose of the millennial reign was for the perfecting of those who were worthy to be present at the coming of our Lord. And, in this process of perfection, to make those who were fully responsive ready to dwell in the presence of God the Father. Joseph Smith, the first prophet of the Restoration, concerned himself a great deal with the subject of Zion and the kingdom of God. He seemed at times to use the words as if they were synonymous, and this is agreeable for our purpose.

I feel that one of the many evidences of the rightness of the divine call of Joseph Smith was the fact that he concerned himself so early in his religious experience with the subject of Zion. A thread of testimony which runs throughout the scriptures witnesses of Zion. Through the efforts of great hymn writers and great poets, there has been kept alive in the hearts of many people the age-old hope of a righteous society which would demonstrate to mankind the values of "peace on earth and good will toward men." As early as 1830, Joseph was inspired to write in regard to the Zion of Enoch (Genesis 6 and Hebrews 11) in what is now Section 36 of the Doctrine and Covenants. It is also found in the seventh chapter of the book of Genesis in the Inspired Version of the Bible. Here partial clarification and perhaps definition of some aspects of Zion are made: "And the Lord called his people Zion, because they were of one heart and of one mind, and dwelt in righteousness; and there was no poor among them" (D. and C. 36:2h, i). "And it came to pass in his days that he built a city that was called a city of holiness, even Zion" (D. and C. 36:3a). In 1831, during a time of persecution, the prophet spoke to the church again and this is recorded in Section 45:13, 14 of the Doctrine and Covenants. Among other things he said,

"And it shall come to pass, among the wicked, that every man that will not take his sword against his neighbor, must needs flee unto Zion for safety. And there shall be gathered unto it out of every nation under heaven; and it shall be the only people that shall not be at war one with another. And it shall be said among the wicked, Let us not go up to battle against Zion, for the inhabitants of Zion are terrible, wherefore we can not stand. And it shall come to pass that the righteous shall be gathered out from among all nations, and shall come to Zion singing, with songs of everlasting joy."

In 1833 a revelation was given at Kirtland, Ohio, shortly after the laying of the cornerstone of the Kirtland Temple. The prophet sought to define Zion again and said, "For this is Zion, the pure in heart." In June of 1834 we find the prophet saying, "And Zion cannot be built up unless it is by the principles of the law of the celestial kingdom."

As the idea of Zion became further clarified, it dealt with many aspects of human relationship. In fact, it became crystal clear that Zion had to do with every facet of human life. It dealt with all that man is and all that he hopes to be in righteous association with his fellows and God.

The idea of the use of temporal goods and properties was injected into the total theory and theology of Zion. Basic to everything else, Zion was to be a great spiritual adventure. Paul Hanson, an apostle for the church, used to say something like this: "Zion is the greatest challenge ever given to the mind of man."

Some have so cumbered the idea of Zion with what is called the temporal aspects that many have said Zion can never be. This, of course, is not so when one sees Zion as basically a spiritual experience and begins to realize that before the kingdom of God (with all of its ramifications) can ever be a reality it must first be born in the heart of man. The complication of temporal aspects begins to fall into its proper relationship to the other aspects of Zion when this spiritually takes place.

The young prophet saw with greater clarity than perhaps he himself realized when he laid down certain postulates. It became evident to him, apparently, that basic to man's achieving Zion and the kingdom of God was the necessity to reach a "one heart and one mind" state which would allow living in righteousness. Also one of the basic requirements was that man love his fellowman so that each, seeking to be of benefit to another, would bring about a condition where there would be no poor among the people. This applies to things other than goods. It applies to those aspects of life which have aesthetic value. The aesthete might have much of this world's goods and still be poor in a very real sense if his need of art and beauty was not satisfied.

Zion also was considered as a place of safety, but apparently many people misunderstood the intent of the revelation. This was not a safety to be meted out to some chosen few regardless of their commitment to the cause of righteousness. There was to be safety in Zion, as there has always been "safety" for men of goodwill in whose hearts is found the spirit of the living Christ. These have known death and physical tribulation but have had a serene sense of safety and well-being regardless of the condition of the physical world about them. The prophet inferred this when he said that Zion was the pure in heart and further that Zion could only be redeemed according to the celestial law.

I see Zion as an endeavor on the part of understanding and dedicated Christians to exemplify the great commandment which was second only to the greatest, that men ought to love others in the same measure that they love themselves. This is opposed to the dog-eat-dog, get-the-other-fellow-first-lest-he-find-some-way-to-take-advantage-of-you, claw-and-shove-and-push-everything-that-gets-in-your-way-to-the-top type of thinking which seems to be in large measure the spirit of the world in every age.

Men shall never, of course, love each other until they have first come to love God—to appreciate something of his love and accept the gifts which he has made available by virtue of his grace. There is no suggestion that the accomplishment of this task shall be easy, nor is there a promise that the way ahead shall be smooth; rather, as one responds to the love of God in extending love to his fellowman, he shall, by God's grace, receive strength and power to overcome the selfishness and the hate which seem to be the common inheritance of mankind.

I had an experience many years ago which made me know that Zion would not be easy to achieve. As I was sitting on the platform during a reunion in western Iowa one Sunday morning, I received one of the few open visions that has been given me. There passed before my eyes, in panoramic view, things which I understood then and now to concern Zion. My experience that morning was this:

> As I looked down a road which appeared before me and began to travel that road, I became aware that there were tremendous obstacles along the way. These were presented to me in the form of rough and tricky terrain

over which I must travel, and in other places there were huge boulders lying in the very center of the path which I had been called to travel. But as I moved with a strength and assurance which came from outside and dwelt within me, I became aware of a city in the distance whose glory defies my ability to describe. The whole community (I was privileged to see it from a high hill that looked out across a vast expanse) seemed to be illuminated with light, power, and a glory that seemed nothing short of divine. How long I was wrapped in the vision I have no way of telling, but since I felt no direction of the Spirit at the time to relate the experience, I held my peace. It was so indelibly impressed on my mind that through the years I have found help when the spiritual terrain has been tricky, the boulders large, and the hills steep. Always there has been available, when the basic requirements of Zion have been present in my life, the sustaining grace of the Holy Spirit.

The very spirit of Zion demands that its expression be felt outside the household of one's own faith. As the spirit of the kingdom is born in his heart, something of the witness of the living Christ must be shared. Those who build or those who redeem Zion will, of course, have to deal with the temporal aspects of life. They will be caught up in the field of commerce (the social and political life of man) from which they cannot extricate themselves.

Stewardship of money, property, time, and talent will be of tremendous importance to one who catches the vision of Zion. But these are seen in proper relationship by those who have sensed clearly that it is the business of the disciples of Jesus to be dispensers of that spirit of oneness for which he prayed in the seventeenth chapter of the gospel of John.

Zion, then, shall be the result of total conversion, a near

complete dedication, as people take unto themselves the benefits of the celestial law and share these benefits and gifts of the Almighty with their fellows. This attitude of mind and spirit can never be known by worldly men and women. It comes only to those who accept the grace of God as they make preparation through the help of God's Spirit to receive and use his gifts properly.

Adventure for Christ

By Gerald and Twyla Fitch

It was the eve of our takeoff date. We were checking and double-checking our list. Luggage and boxes were packed and repacked as our bathroom scales told us we were too heavy for Tri-pacer 3041Z. Early the next morning 41Z climbed out, we dipped a wing to our office assistant as she waved good-bye from the back porch, and then trimmed out southwest. The morning haze soon closed the curtain on Plymouth, Michigan. Telephones and appointments were exchanged for charts, omnis, and the anticipation of an untried clinic in Mexico. Three days marked with stops for fuel, comfort, and lodging moved us uneventfully to Monterrey, Mexico, forty-five miles from Saltillo, our destination, with a storm in the pass daring us to continue. After three hours on the ground, a local pilot, surveying the sky with narrowed eyes and wrinkled forehead, thought we could now make it through, assuring us further that we could always turn back. With this send-off we climbed to the 6,000 ceiling and followed over the highway into the pass. The mountains on either side top out at 12,000 and the highway ascends to

56

something over 5,500. With a three- to four-mile visibility, this, as any flyer knows, left me looking for a keyhole in the sky and a wife giving me plenty of advice. The previous uneventfulness, to say the least, became duly colored. Surviving the estimated twenty minutes we slipped through, 400 to 500 feet above the road's summit, out into a beautiful, cloudless sky with Saltillo's runway dead ahead.

We had made many trips to Mexico during the past fourteen years, but the most interesting one was occurring in the month of May, 1966. It all began when Seventy Robert Fishburn had assured us that dental care for the students at Restaumex Student Center was needed and would be a fine contribution. Immediately we had begun to collect equipment and supplies for a portable clinic. The dental salesmen who call at our office brought us a good set of elevators and forceps. The Christian Dental Society contributed other instruments, a sterilizer, and portable cabinet; dental supply companies supplied us with anesthetic and disposable needles. Now, miles from the office, we were landing in Saltillo, Mexico.

The suspense of the flight was soon forgotten as Harold Smith, director of the Restaumex Student Center, drove us to the former governor's mansion which now serves as the headquarters for the church in Saltillo. The greeting and welcome from our good friends, the Fishburns, put us at ease and at home. The next day students and all gave a hand as our equipment was carried to the third floor where we were assigned a room for our clinic. Long will we remember the stained-glass windows as we upped the stairs and took our first look at the city below and the mountains beyond. This was our penthouse clinic for twelve interesting days.

With our equipment on location, Twyla busied herself unpacking and sterilizing while I went to the former carriage house (now a storage room) to improvise an aged kitchen chair into a dental chair. By lashing a length of board to the chair's back with a pillow tied on top for a headrest and using the top of Saltillo's first RLDS pulpit for a platform to give the chair more height, plus two lengths of 2 x 4's to regulate the height up and down, we had a chair that worked quite well. The hanging of large illustrated dental care charts on the walls and receiving permission to work from the Mexican public health put the clinic in final order. The portable drill was lifted from its hook and the old familiar tune was played. The end of an interesting week found us well acquainted with thirty interesting and appreciative students, plus twenty members of the local congregation who had received twenty-three fillings and sixteen extractions. Each received a toothbrush and a tube of toothpaste, with personal instructions on how to use them! We were well paid for the effort by the expressions of appreciation from this fine group. As I told one student in my poor Spanish (who tried to tell me in equally poor English how he appreciated this dental care), "Because I see that you appreciate this, Jesus has already paid me in my heart." The smile that followed was a good fee.

Having completed our work with the students at Restaumex, we invited Reverend and Mrs. Northrup of the Christian Church to bring ten students from their school. As we worked and visited with this fine group, we learned that Reverend Northrup made two trips each week 160 miles south into the mountains to minister. He told us of the dental needs in this area, and we arranged to go with him and take our extraction instruments and improvised chair.

Our ride out and back in a small truck is beyond description. We visited three primitive villages, Sandia Grande, Soledad, and La Trinidad, where we set up our clinic under the trees, using a card table, a portable cabinet and suitcase, a galvanized bucket for boiling our instruments on a rock furnace—and our faithful chair. Reverend Northrup went among the grass houses inviting those with toothaches to come and see the dentist for one peso. A crowd soon assembled—some with aches, some with curiosity. We worked until no more stood in line and moved on to the next village where we set up our makeshift clinic in their new, one-room schoolhouse. We worked well into the night by flashlight.

The honesty and appreciation of these good people is reflected in a knock that came on the schoolhouse door during our work that night. Opening the door we were greeted by a small boy, maybe ten years old, who smiled and extended his hand. In it lay a peso from his mother who had had an extraction in the first village six miles back. She had had a tooth that needed extracting but no peso. She had promised to pay when her husband came in from the field, and our little Abe Lincoln had brought it the six miles to "settle the debt." After giving us the money, the little boy ran off into the night for the six-mile journey home. Many other interesting episodes will long be ours to enjoy. There was the lady who paid with a chicken and the man who said we could have his goat if we would take out all his teeth. When the last patient was treated, we gladly bedded down for a deserved rest.

Our rest in the schoolhouse ended the next morning when the people suggested it was time to work by pecking on the window and announcing that they had toothaches. They had missed us the preceding day in the former village and had followed us to the schoolhouse. Our canned breakfast was quickly over and the routine was again clicking. By early afternoon, we depleted the line at the third village.

In this two-day adventure we registered a total of 96 extractions in an area that is 35 oxcart miles from dental service ... which is only part time if at all. Negotiating the

160 miles back to Saltillo was a jolly trip. We felt good over our very successful clinic.

Our adventures had put greater significance into the scripture which tells us "it is greater to give than to receive," but all things must come to an end. The time for good-byes had arrived. We loaded our equipment back onto the Tri-pacer and, amid wishes for good visibility in the pass, headed for home.

Our two-day flight to Michigan via 41Z was uneventful. The richest experience of our lives was finished. One of our colleagues was quick to say it would have been no vacation for him to go and work. Our reply was that this was the nearest thing to eating our cake and still having it that we knew. No pay could be greater than this feeling in our hearts.

Never Too Late

Anonymous

I drove by the establishment. Everything seemed to be normal; the night-lights were on and the neighborhood was quiet. The only problem was a place to park.

I parked across the street from the building. There wasn't another car on the street—and this was bad. I knew it was dangerous, but it was the only place within a reasonable distance. But my luck had been good, and I took the chance that the car would not be under suspicion.

Gathering my tools and crouching, I left the car noiselessly and ran across the lighted street. I stopped in the shadows beside the building. I scanned the neighborhood, and finding it still quiet, efficiently broke the glass out of a window, taking care to remove all the pieces from the pane.

I checked again to be sure that no one had been aroused, then I slipped into the building. It took only a moment to force the office door. I found the company safe which was a large one and fairly new.

As quietly as possible, I went to work on the safe door, stopping periodically to look outside. When I was about half through, I saw a squad car coming down the street. I've had it, I thought. The cop will easily see the damaged safe from the street. With my car parked out there, he's sure to look.

Gathering up what tools were handy, I ran from the office as headlights from the police car filled it with light.

I made my way rapidly through the dark building. Suddenly I found myself falling down a short flight of stairs. It seemed hours before I could function again, although I knew it was but a few seconds.

I found a side door at the bottom of the stairs. I unlocked it and opened it a crack. It was clear. The cop was still in front of the building. I ran out of the building.

A dog began to bark in front of two houses which I'd planned to go between. I was cut off. The only way remaining was across the railroad track and into an open field.

I had just reached the tracks when the police car pulled around the side of the building. I dove to the tracks and tried to hide behind the steel rails.

The dog was barking and making such a commotion I was afraid it would arouse the cop's suspicion. The headlights of the police car passed over me as he drove beside the building. This is it, I thought. The car stopped. The policeman played the spotlight over the back of the building and then, to my amazement, he turned the patrol car around and drove back to the front.

As I lay there watching and waiting, he pulled in behind

my car. He got out of the patrol car and walked around my car shining his light inside. Finally, he returned to his car and drove off. He had the license number and a description of my car.

I rose to my feet and went back into the building. I finished working over the safe, collected the money, my tools, and returned to my car. As I drove out of town, I drove past the policeman who had checked the building. He didn't stop my car.

As I drove home I thought how fortunate I had been. Too much had happened in my favor to be just blind luck. The cop should have seen the broken glass on the ground. He should have seen the safe half battered open. He should have seen me behind the tracks. And he should have stopped my car as I left town, but he didn't. No, this couldn't have been luck; there had been too much against me.

I should have been dead, but I was alive. My plan for self-destruction was to burglarize and steal until I was caught. Then I would "hold court in the street"–that is, fight it out with the police and not be taken alive. Being an ex-convict I knew what prison life was—and I wasn't going back.

I welcomed the thought of death. I felt that I was without hope in this life. I had been trapped in a hopeless marriage and now even that was gone. I was nearly cut off from my children. I had had my fill of life. The only way to peace seemed to be in death.

I couldn't attribute this "luck" to God or an act of God because I was an atheist. I didn't believe in God. I believed that when a person died it was the end—the total of his existence. With a philosophy like this, I was free to do anything and everything I pleased.

The next day I read an account of the burglary in the paper. The police theorized that three or four persons were

62

involved and that a car parked near the scene was probably not implicated.

A few days after the burglary I received a call from a woman who had been my Sunday school teacher. She said, among other things in her conversation, "You can have the peace that you so earnestly long for."

Those few words jarred me. For the rest of the day they bothered me. Even when I went to bed I was unable to sleep, haunted by them. I tossed in torment many hours before I became aware that the room was filled with a Presence other than my own. A Spirit became so strong that I trembled, and was unable to control it.

In that moment I knew there was a God and that that which I had been taught in my childhood was true. "It's too late!" I cried out. "My life is too messed up! There's no hope." But that Spirit would not let me rest, and I found hope in that fact. Maybe it wasn't too late. I said, "God, if you will help me put my life in order, I'll serve you." With this submission came the knowledge that if I would put sin out of my life I would be blessed above all my anticipations.

The next day I found lawful employment.

Later in the week I kept an appointment that I had made with my former Sunday school teacher. Her contribution to my spiritual growth at this time was unmeasurable. The next Sunday I went to church for the first time in many years. I wished that it had been possible to sneak in the back door and sit through the service unnoticed. Yet I felt that this was my place, the place where I belonged. The Saints in the branch received me without question and with open arms.

At a time such as this one needs spiritual guidance, so one evening I called on the pastor. I told him of my recent criminal activity and my marital problems and, again, I found much help. He spoke a great yet simple truth—the church is for sinners.

The Sunday following was Easter. As I sat in church, I thought how nice it would be if I could eat dinner and fellowship with one of the Saints. I considered praying about it but decided it was too small a matter to bring before the Lord. Just as I thought these thoughts a woman came to me and invited me to dinner. I thanked God for answering a prayer that I had not prayed.

At dinner I was made to feel at home with members of the family. After dinner, I went bowling with the woman's stepson. He and I became good friends.

I had been praying about my marriage and God's will for it. Yet each time I visited my wife, she became more distant. Then one day, as I prayed, a feeling of peace came over me, and I knew that the matter was settled. I went to see her, and she ordered me out of the house.

A short time later my wife divorced me. In the meantime I had met a woman, the daughter of my former Sunday school teacher, who had been divorced. I didn't know her too well, but I felt that we needed each other. I made up my mind to speak to her about how I felt. That evening I drove to her home, but I was relieved to find her car gone, for it gave me an excuse to delay.

As I drove away, however, I was seized with an overwhelming compulsion to speak to her as if it had to be at this time. I drove to her mother's, thinking she might be there, but she wasn't.

I drove back to her house determined to see her. This time her car was parked in front of the apartment house.

I parked my car and sat behind the wheel a few moments, praying that God would give me the words that I must say and the strength to speak them. I entered the house and stopped about halfway up the stairs. I could see an open door above me. I knocked as loudly as I could on the bannister. There was no response. I did not want to confront her at an open door. I wasn't even sure that she would remember me. I was about to retreat down the stairs when a door opened in the hall below. Her two children came into the hall wearing pajamas.

"Who are you?" the little boy asked.

"Mommy, there's a man here," the little girl called.

She came out behind the children and said, "Well, John, hello!" She had remembered my name.

She was quite attractive. After some conversation she invited me into the apartment and made me feel comfortable. I told her my divorce had been granted that day. We had soft drinks and the kids sat on my lap. She began to tell me about her work at the state mental hospital. The more she talked the more unsure I became. Boy, I thought, she's going to think I'm some kind of a nut. I considered leaving.

Around nine she hinted that it was getting late and she had to get up early. I knew that I must speak or lose the opportunity forever. I lacked courage for a second try.

"I'd like to speak to you," I managed to say. She understood that I wanted to speak in private so she put the children to bed.

When she returned to the living room and sat down I began. "I felt directed to come here this evening," I said. "I think that God wishes for us to marry. If you are interested and will pray about it, I am sure you will receive the same knowledge." Her expression did not become hostile, and I took courage.

"You must understand that there are things in my life that you should know about," I continued. "I'm an ex-convict. I've done a five-year sentence for burglary."

"That doesn't make any difference. You've paid your debt to society."

"I'll help you rear your children the way they should be reared."

65

"I'm sure that you would."

"I honestly believe I could love them as I love my own. And I love my children very much."

"I know that you do. I've seen you and your boys in church, and I know by the way you act with them that you love them."

"I can't say that I love you. I don't know you."

"Well, no," she said.

"But I'm sure love will come if we are concerned. It's late, and I had better go. If you pray about this I'm sure you'll get an answer."

"I'll pray about it," she promised.

"I'll try not to bother you until you have an answer. I don't want to influence you. Good-night," I said as I made my way to the hall.

"Good-night," she replied as she closed the door.

I got into my car and sat behind the wheel a few minutes thanking God that my words were received in the same faith that they were given and thanking him for his Spirit which had been with me. As I drove home I felt ten feet tall in the knowledge that she would be my wife.

An evening or two later, I began to doubt the wisdom of this proposed marriage. I thought of the mess my first marriage had been, and wondered if I should even try again. As I thought of these things, the Spirit came over me with such force that I was driven to my knees. I didn't doubt the wisdom of it again.

A week went by and I hadn't received an answer from her. I had felt that I was in love with her. I began to worry. What would I do if she didn't get an answer or chose not to marry me? It was ten days from the day I spoke to her that she, through fasting and praying, received the same light. We were married May 26, 1966.

I have been blessed. I never dreamed that life could be so

sweet. Even the word wife has taken on a new meaning; it has become a word full of warmth and love, as indeed she is.

It is never too late to accept Jesus Christ as savior and live by his teachings unless we ourselves make it too late by rejecting the call to repentance. I have had many wonderful blessings, yet I wish I could say as the apostle Paul, "I have fought the good fight and lived the good life."

It seems sad to me that the most important decision that people have to make is often made without the aid of the Lord. I am sure that if anyone asks God about marriage God will guide that person as he has guided us. A marriage ordained and blessed by God should not fail.

I have known many professional criminals. I've worked with a few and did time with many. All of them, to a man, know that sooner or later they'll be caught; they play the odds as an occupational hazard. They have a saying, "If you can't do the time, don't do the crime."

There is no pleasure in telling the person you wish to marry that you're an ex-convict or that you have been in trouble. Before you become a party to any foolish act, think! Think of how it will affect you the rest of your life. Don't make the mistake of becoming a second-class citizen. You will carry any record that you make the rest of your life. Nothing wipes the slate clean. You will always be an ex-con.

Gospel of Joy

By Donald D. Landon

Christian scholars have been interested in the many paintings done on the walls of the catacombs in Rome by first-century Christian refugees. These catacombs, really subterranean cemeteries, served as secret meeting places for the Christian community during the time of persecution. The paintings are frequently representations of the person of Christ. What amazes us is the conception of Jesus conveyed in them. Each carries a magnificent spirit of joy. Regardless of their refugee status and all the suffering entailed in their persecuted discipleship, the joy the gospel brought to these first-century Christians broke through all the gloom of their circumstances.

These crude paintings are the believers' own testimony that what the angel chorus declared to the Judean shepherds at the birth of Christ was true. The tidings were of great joy, and were for all people. Not only did the early believers witness to their joy in subterranean paintings but their literature carries a persistent theme of rejoicing. The New Testament spreads a contagion of gladness. It repeats the admonition, "Be of good cheer." So characteristic was this gladsomeness of the early believers that the book of Barnabas speaks of Christians as "the children of joy." A veritable ethos of rapture permeated the community.

While attending a university I became acquainted with a Hindu student from India. He had never read the Christian New Testament, so I invited him to read through it and share his impressions with me. Some months later he wrote me from another city where he had finished the reading. He said, "I find two things most impressive. First, the stark realism found on every page. Nothing about man is hidden or softened. But then, in the midst of this harsh realism there is a pervasive joy which radiates unmistakably from the verses. It seems to arrest the very heart of a man. I find it difficult to get free of it."

Jesus definitely considered his mission as the invoking of gladness into hearts parched under the relentless torture of sin, purposelessness, and uncertainty. Luke declares that "he went throughout every city and village, preaching and showing the glad tidings of the kingdom of God." One of the last things Jesus said to his disciples was, "These things have I spoken unto you, that my joy might remain in you, and that your joy might be full."

Would anyone coming into our churches today discover a people who feel they have made a glorious discovery, and are thrilled, and joy-possessed? Is there contemporary awareness that the gospel means good news? Does our preaching convey the exuberance of one who has found a treasure? Would a visitor in our midst discover joy, optimism, faith, and confidence as the common denominator of our lives?

While the message of the gospel is as broad as all of life's experiences, it nevertheless carries one fundamental theme— the good news of God's action for our salvation. This good news is the provision which God has made in Christ for the salvation and transformation of the life of mankind. It includes the means by which the true relation between God and man might be restored.

It is easy in an age like ours which is so vulnerable to the attacks of moralists to spend one's time giving good advice. But the fact is that the gospel is not essentially good advice. It doesn't begin by telling people they ought to be good. Rather does it begin by saying that God is good; so good, in fact, that while we were helpless, he acted for our salvation.

Maybe the reason the gospel hasn't seemed good news to many is that too often it has been presented as advice on how to swim to a man who is overboard in the middle of the Atlantic Ocean. Somehow, such advice is simply irrelevant to the situation. No improvement of technique is going to enable a man to swim thousands of miles to land. What he needs is a salvation outside himself. This is the good news of the gospel. It is the saving action of God to which we can respond in faith. This is why Paul can say, "I am not ashamed of the gospel of Christ: for it is the power of God unto salvation to every one that believeth" (Romans 1:16).

The good news of God's undiscouraged love, his unmerited forgiveness, his breaking the bonds of death for our sake, his invitation to sit with him as his children—all these facts somehow change the circumstances of our life. It isn't exactly that by the gospel we see different things; rather is it that we see *things* differently.

I am reminded of an elderly woman in Sweden whose life has been transformed by the joy of the gospel. She has never known good health. Her twisted and pain-wracked body has been a burden heavy enough to dull the eyes and depress the soul of the most courageous. But every visit I made to her evidenced that the gospel has brought joy into her life which is impervious even to her ill health. She is an assured person. The love of God is more real to her than her twisted hands. Her fellowship with her Redeemer is experienced more deeply than the pain of her tortured back. Her inner resource of joy can never be touched by the passing things of this world, including handicap and pain.

This woman is something like the peasant farmer of whom Jesus spoke. Bent under the unremitting toil of making ends meet, he finds his strength steadily absorbed in trying to wrest a living from the earth. Then one day he happens to plow somewhat deeper than is customary and comes upon a hidden treasure in the field. With his discovery, his poverty is over and he has entered upon a richness he never dreamed possible (Matthew 13:44).

Such is the kingdom of heaven. To know the gospel is to discover a treasure of joy which casts all things in a new light. If we do not know the gospel as a message of joy, we are defrauding ourselves of the major portion of the gift that God intends for us. If our lives are not buoyed up and lifted

70

above the reefs upon which so many lives end as shipwrecks, somehow we've missed the content of the gospel (II Timothy 1:10). When Jesus declared that he was come that we might have life and have it more abundantly (John 10:10), he was asserting that life derives its fullest meaning when lived within the context of the gospel. This context includes the love of God for man, the forgiveness of sins, the adoption of repentant persons into the family of God, the projection of life beyond death, the reality of the kingdom, and a host of other joy-giving facts.

There are so many things that seek to deprive us of the full joy of the gospel. God faithfully sows the seed of the good news before us. But often it falls by the wayside of our lives, is never given the attention and understanding it deserves, and thus is lost to us by default. Other times the gospel falls on a heart that is skeptical. It may take some root, but the soil of trust is not deep enough to let it mature, and before long the good news has wilted under the relentless attacks of doubt.

There are some hearts in which the good news is sown which are already so filled with concerns, commitments, and cares which are hostile to the gospel that the young sprout is soon choked out by the thorns.

Hopefully, our hearts can be as deep soil, broken and prepared for the seed. In such an environment of faith and understanding the good news takes root and blesses its host with joy unspeakable.

An Affirmative Answer

By Lily Oakman

Acceptance of the Book of Mormon as scripture was part of my heritage as a third-generation Latter Day Saint by both of my parents in the Reorganized Church. My first real acquaintance with the book was in my early teens, when my sister and I were allowed the privilege of sitting in an adult class which my father taught in our home. We "read round" in the good old-fashioned way and discussed what we had read, and from this exercise there was no doubt in my mind that the book was of divine origin.

As I matured I became aware of some of the reasons why people outside the church did not accept the Book of Mormon as scripture. These did not worry me very much until I became personally acquainted in my business life with those of other Christian denominations who did not accept the divine origin of the book, and told me so in plain terms. As I realized what a large body of opinion held this view, it concerned me very much and I felt the need for a personal testimony that the book was what it claimed to be.

I prayed earnestly for such a testimony, but without any preconceived notion of what form it should take—leaving this in the hands of God. I had little personal acquaintance with the content of the book, preferring for my scripture study the Pauline Epistles and the Doctrine and Covenants, which had more immediate appeal to me than the long, and what seemed to me then, tedious chapters of the Book of Mormon.

In time I forgot my prayer for this testimony—in fact, it faded from my mind for some years. I was quite satisfied as to the divinity of the restored church from my experiences with God in it, and also a deep personal study of the New Testament, comparing its teachings with those of the Reorganized Church, and both of these with the teachings of other Christian denominations as I came in contact with their ideas. Yet God did answer my prayer, in a simple yet unexpected way.

The Enfield Branch had a pastor, Elder J. Franklin

Schofield, who used the Book of Mormon in public worship much more than any other pastor I remember. In one service I was listening intently to his reading when the voice of the Spirit of God whispered to my innermost consciousness, "Is not this good and true? Does it not invite men and women to follow Jesus Christ and his righteousness? Is it not of God?" The conviction entered into the very depths of my soul that the answer to the questions was in the affirmative. Then, quick as a flash, came the remembrance of my prayer, and the realization that this was its answer! I would emphasize that at the time I had no question in my mind concerning the Book of Mormon, nor any remembrance of my prayer of some years previously.

Since that experience I have read the Book of Mormon for myself a great deal and obtained further testimony from its "internal evidence." I have thrilled to the clarity and purity of the gospel teachings it contains, followed the fortunes of the people of God through the various vicissitudes of its history, and shared the sorrow of its great prophets who warned their people of the dangers of forgetting God. I am satisfied that these writings were not concocted out of the imagination of a man with intent to deceive, or by one who suffered from hallucinations, for I have allowed my mind to consider these possibilities, and I have tried to read the book from the point of view of one who would think this way. But it just does not fit that category.

I am aware of some of the difficulties in the way of a modern theological scholar accepting the book as scripture. I know also that there are differences of opinion as to the manner of Joseph Smith's translation, whether the actual wording was given to him or whether the sense was given and he clothed it in his own language. None of these considerations, however, can refute the sublime nature of the teachings of the Book of Mormon in inviting men and women to come to Christ, the soundness of its moral principles, its clear and plain exposition of gospel truths, its solid backing of much of biblical narrative, and above all, its undergirding of the claim of Christ to be the Only Begotten Son of God and the Savior of the world.

These are my reasons for believing the Book of Mormon to be of divine origin—a "marvelous work and a wonder"—and positive evidence of the truth of the Restoration story.

Faces of Many People

By Wilbur C. Mattes

In the summer of 1964 my pastor, Lester Hunt of Tabor, Iowa, informed me that I had been called to the office of priest in the Aaronic priesthood. I had not expected the call and was quite surprised.

Yet, during the preceding week while I was working in my fields, the thought repeatedly came to me—"What would you do if you were called to serve in the priesthood?" At each occurrence I would brush away the thought as if it were an impossibility. I felt (even though I had a deep desire to be of service) that I would never be able to fulfill the requirements. I was not able to comprehend or absorb all the thoughts which went through my mind concerning the responsibility, my lack of knowledge, my unworthiness, my weakness, my many mistakes of the past—my lack of everything needed to fill a call to such service. Still, however, there was the willingness, the long-burning desire to be of some help to others and to be of good service to the Master.

Brother Hunt explained that he had received sufficient evidence for my calling. He also advised me to take a few days to think and pray about it. Before he left our home, the Spirit of God bore heavily upon me. I was so deeply impressed I told him that if the Lord had a work for me to do, I could not refuse.

But upon retiring, the question "What could God possibly want with me?" rested so heavily upon my mind that I could not sleep. After struggling with this question (for nothing else could enter my mind) I was taken in a vision to the steps of our church in Tabor. As I stood there shaking the hands of three elders who had just ordained me to the office of priest, I turned and looked out upon a field which covered a valley and a hillside. The field was filled with a multitude of people. They all had their faces turned toward me and were looking at me in such way as to reveal that they were waiting for me to lead them, teach them, guide them—and pray for them. Thus the answer to my question, "What could God possibly want with me?"

The time of day in the vision bothers me. It must have distinct meaning. It was late in the day—just before dusk. It was light enough to see each face clearly, but I sensed that the day was growing short. Since I was fifty years of age, I wondered if this meant that my time for rendering service was growing short. To my mind came the words of Section 142 of the Doctrine and Covenants, "It is yet day when all can work. The night will come when for many of my people opportunity to assist will have passed."

My ordination did not take place for several months, at which time the three elders instead of the usual two officiated as was shown me in the vision.

This experience will always be dear to me. The Lord answered my prayer. He confirmed my calling and showed concern for me. Therefore I will need to walk close to the

Master, to study to understand the scriptures, to stand firmly in his church. I must lift burdens, unlock hearts that are not in harmony with his, smile, forgive, pray, hold high the light of Christ, love as he has loved me.

I shall never be satisfied with my limited knowledge and understanding. I want to grow in service worthy of Him who gave me life—who had patience to wait all these long years. He has promised to provide his Spirit to be with me if I but serve with determined effort and faith to the best of my ability.

As I strive to meet the requirements of a priest I find many of the eager faces and they respond well. Truly "the fields are white and ready to harvest."

The Gift of Awareness

By James M. Wilkinson

I was reared in the church by a kind and loving family in Independence, Missouri. On reaching the age of accountability I was baptized, confirmed, and fully capable of choosing between righteousness or rebellion. I chose the latter and soon found myself at odds with my family and friends. This attitude led to teen-age mischief and willful harm to property and the lives of loved ones, and eventually a move away from Independence.

I continued in this life of prideful rebellion through high school, military service, and one year of college. I found worldly success temporarily in local business, travel, and political life; but I became increasingly irresponsible with finances and soon found myself deep in debt.

In loneliness I sought companionship and married a lovely young woman. My rebellion continued through the early months of our marriage and through several jobs. Under these conditions our heavenly Father granted us a fine little girl. For the first time in my life I found myself unable to provide for my family and unfit to be a father.

While employed as a traveling salesman for a small manufacturing firm, I found myself in Oklahoma City on that fateful day, November 22, 1963. I had identified with the political ideals of President Kennedy and was stunned by the realization of his assassination. I turned to my Father in despair.

On that day in my motel room in Oklahoma City, out of the love of God—his grace, his condescension—and through the gift of the Holy Spirit, I was granted an awareness of my relationship to him. This gift of awareness turned me to the local branch of our church. I bought a copy of the Inspired Version of the Bible, a Book of Mormon, and a Doctrine and Covenants. I began to study the word of God. As I studied I sought repentance and reconciliation to my heavenly Father through his Only Begotten Son. I found rest, hope, and forgiveness. I shared this experience with my wife and family and began to order my life in accordance with the principles of the gospel.

I share with you the testimony that Jesus Christ is the Only Begotten Son of our heavenly Father; that he lives and is ever ready to reach out in loving concern for the children of men; that he has restored his gospel in the latter days; that he calls men to stand in his stead on earth through his holy priesthood; that this priesthood authority resides in Christ's church. And finally, that through the sacraments and ordinances of Christ's church and the gift of his Holy Spirit, man is granted the opportunity to grow unto righteousness, for he has said, "I am the way, the truth, and the life; no man cometh unto the Father but by me."

If You Truly Repent

By Lillian Black

I was born in Kansas City, Missouri, on May 30, 1914. I was baptized into the church in 1927. I believed in God as my heavenly Father and Jesus Christ as my Savior.

I left the RLDS Church through a misunderstanding when I was fifteen. Soon after, I married a member of the Roman Catholic faith. We had three daughters.

My husband died when I was nineteen and I reared the children in the Catholic faith until their first communion. About this time I moved to another neighborhood and we joined the Methodist Church.

I went my own merry way for years. I remarried and became a widow two more times and one marriage ended in divorce. I did various things to earn a livelihood, including operating three taverns, working in a car auction, owning a car lot and ice-cream parlor, and selling real estate. I had much happiness—and at times many hardships. I stopped going to any church. I was too busy. I prayed to God for help when I needed it and he never let me down. He did all for me—and I did nothing for him.

My children married into various faiths. I thought I had been very wise in arranging their lives so that it wouldn't matter who they married or what church they attended. I told myself it wasn't necessary to go to any church even though I still believed in God and Christ and in such things as faith and repentance. "Besides, look at all the hypocrites in church," I would say. (I had had two different "preachers" ask me to go in with them to start a church for the money in it. It was good business, they said, when you could get 10 percent of the salaries of those who came into the church.)

I always tried to repent when I did something wrong, often consciously asking for forgiveness several times for the same thing. I told God I was sorry, but I kept doing wrong. I know *true* repentance now. It isn't just a momentary flash of "I'm sorry, Lord." True repentance is deep sorrow. Your "heart" breaks from a knowledge of sins; your eyes flow with tears as you see your entire life in review.

In 1963 I had difficulties physically, beginning with an operation for adhesions. I had known sickness throughout my life, but this was different. I would recover from one operation only to find it necessary to have another. I had five serious operations in three years. Both my life and my husband's life were miserable.

A friend who had had the same difficulties visited me and told me that she had not had surgery in four years. She also claimed that the Lord had healed her. I listened respectfully but doubted her words. My sister Dorothy was a member of the RLDS Church and she also begged me to ask for administration (laying on of hands for the sick). I told her that I didn't believe in such nonsense, that I would do my own praying and didn't need anyone to pray for me.

Then I was brought to my knees. I had a serious car accident in December 1966. I went into shock and was unable to eat. For nine months the doctors performed surgery to correct the condition, but to no avail. Finally (I had been home from the hospital only a few days) I called my doctor, and he said that he could do no more for me. I was too weak for more surgery. The doctor had given me up to die.

My husband was out of town and in this situation I found myself alone. I started praying—this time really praying for God to tell me what to do. Peculiar thoughts went through my head. I did not want to be buried without a minister. I thought of my deceased brother, and of his minister who was a Baptist. I liked this minister and wondered if he would come. I thought of my next-door neighbor and I wondered if she would call her minister for me. I had to do something. I couldn't be buried without a minister. I hadn't been going to any church. I had strayed so far. Then suddenly I remembered that I had been baptized into the Reorganized Church of Jesus Christ of Latter Day Saints. Out of my jumbled thoughts came the idea to call my sister, Dorothy, and ask her to bring the elders.

I worked my way to the phone as fast as I could. I had lost fifty pounds and was so weak I could scarcely walk. But I was no longer alone; God was with me. I called Dorothy and she told me to have faith, that I was not going to die. She would bring the elders from the church to administer to me—not to talk about officiating at my burial. Soon Brothers Eugene Walton and Joseph Sandidge came to my home. The man named Walton talked to me about God. He asked me if I believed in God and if I had faith that He could heal me. He asked if I was willing to serve the Lord, keeping his commandments and dedicating my life to him, if he saw fit to heal me. He explained that it would be by the grace of God and his blessings alone, through the laying on of the hands, if I were healed. He made it very clear that it was by God's mercy and power and not that of the administering elders. I agreed to do as Brother Walton said and silently made a covenant with God that if he would heal me I would forever do his will and obey his commandments.

I told Brother Walton that I had been a sinner and wanted to be forgiven. I was in need of deep repentance from the life I had led. I told him how alone and empty I had felt; I had been on the wrong side of the fence and not walking with God.

He assured me that if I truly repented and kept the covenant I had just made with Him, to go back into the RLDS Church and live a true Christian life, God would forgive me all my past sins.

After our talk and a prayer the elders administered to me. I have never felt anything in my life like the feeling which went through my body. This was the power of God. I relaxed completely. Tears flowed uncontrolled from my eyes. I wanted to shout the glory of God, for I was instantly healed. The nausea left me and I felt strength flowing through my body. I have never returned to the doctor, and I have not taken any medicine. I am happier and healthier than I have been for years.

Since I was healed I have given myself to the Lord. His desires control my mind, my thoughts, and my body. My every thought seems to center on my covenant. I am deeply thankful for God's blessing and the new way of life I have found.

The Testimony of a Patriarch

By Alan Kelley

I was ordained to be a patriarch-evangelist in April 1967, but for more than ten years preceding the Lord had blessed me with the knowledge that this would come to pass. From the organization of the Tulsa District in the early 1950's, I served as the district bishop's agent. During my ten-year tenure in this position, there were many (including my own mother) who thought I would ultimately be called to be a bishop, but the Lord and I knew different. The knowledge did not come, however, through one great and mighty experience but by the calm witness and assurance of the Holy Spirit through many experiences of ministry.

As a young man in my mid-twenties, I had received wise counsel in my own patriarchal blessing. The patriarch who gave it to me said, in part, "If thou shalt desire it enough and art faithful, thou shalt be pointed out by the spirit of revelation and thou shalt minister as a Melchisedec priest. But let this be as God wills. Ask it not as an advertisement of your desires, but be faithful and humble, and the Lord will seek thee out." It was ten years after this blessing experience before I understood the meaning of the term "Melchisedec priest" and then another eight years before I was called and ordained a high priest.

I have served as an Aaronic priest, an elder, a high priest, and I am now trying to serve as a patriarch. I am more aware than ever before, however, of the fundamental truth that "office in priesthood is not conferred to increase the importance of an individual person, and all offices of the priesthood are of equal honor before God."

In addition to the preceding, there are two specific experiences which seem relevant in my being a patriarch. The first occurred in Tulsa, Oklahoma, late in December of 1961. I lived only fifteen blocks from my work which made it convenient to walk and ideal for physical exercise and spiritual meditation. These walks not only exercised the muscles but also cleared the cobwebs from the mind and permitted the development of new ideas for better ministry. One day I was walking to work early in the morning. It was a beautiful day, cold and crisp and clear. I was glad to be alive. All that was within me was crying out, "My God, how wonderful thou art." I looked into the beauty of the heavens and said aloud, "Great God of the universe, how marvelous is thy creation." Immediately my understanding was quickened to comprehend my words. To my mind came the thought, "My son, it mattereth not whether you live in Tulsa, or in Houston, or in New Orleans, or in Denver, or anywhere else; the only thing that really matters is that you are my servant." I recognized this to be a message of universal truth. A warm feeling of the Holy Spirit sank deep within my very being. A conscious awareness of God's nearness brought unspeakable joy and gladness to my soul.

A year or so before this experience I had had some concern and anxiety about a possible move because of changes in the organization of the company for which I worked. At the time of the experience related these fears had all but disappeared. Then, at midmorning of the day of the experience, the controller of the company called a special meeting of all employees in my department and announced that it was being closed and moved to Houston, Texas. There was no panic for me. I was prepared. The same warm glow within that had brought much joy and gladness a few hours before now brought serenity and peace that was more than ordinary. It brought strong assurance that all is well in the hands of the Infinite Love, and that he was mindful of me and, therefore, mindful of each and every one of his creation.

My second experience would be better named a series of related events that constitute a prelude to my calling as a patriarch. In moving to Houston, and the automatic release from rather heavy priesthood responsibilities in Tulsa, it seemed that the way might be open for the patriarchal ministry about which I had received divine knowledge and assurance. The way was being opened—but not as I might have expected. Within two months after moving to Houston, the district president asked if I were willing to serve as pastor of the Post Oak Branch. He felt it expedient and imperative that I do so. I did not know the people, nor did the people know me. My secular work was new and demanding. Under these circumstances I did not want to be pastor. Yet the spiritual experience regarding our move to Houston would not allow me to refuse. I was not a strong administrator, but I feel that my ministry as pastor for a three-year period was needed and was somewhat effective.

Six months later while driving home alone from the 1966 World Conference, I found myself reflecting upon the possible benefits of early retirement at the age of sixty, then seven years away. Many things came to mind that seemed personally desirable, including priesthood activities. After I had mentally charted a feasible course, I suddenly realized what I was thinking and spoke aloud, "I am saying, Lord, that I will do for you what I want to do, when I want to do it, how I want to do it, and where I want to do it. But this just cannot be." Then, with the humility that comes when one is confronted by the spirit of truth, I said again out loud, "Lord, if it is expedient and necessary for the total good of thy work, I will serve again as pastor of any of the branches in the East Texas District or anywhere else. Furthermore, if such service for the total good means that I will never function as a father and patriarch of your church, it will be all right. I will accept and understand without complaint." A year later I was ordained a patriarch. The apostle who initiated the call told me later that he had received divine direction during our association at the Texas Reunion in June of 1966, which was only two months after I had learned again (while driving home from Conference) that "the only thing that really matters is that you are my servant."

Many who knew me personally before my ordination as a patriarch sought me out for spiritual counsel, but I have been amazed at those who have come for patriarchal ministry and

84

not for the patriarch himself. I am, indeed, keenly aware that office in priesthood is not conferred to increase the importance of one's own self. All calls to priesthood are of equal honor and come because of God's intent to provide ministry for his people.

A Call to Strength

By W. Wallace Smith

In more than two decades of service in the ministry of the church under General Conference appointment (serving three years in the Council of Twelve, eight years as counselor to the President, and now over twelve years as President of the High Priesthood and of the Church), I have been blessed many times by the good Spirit of our heavenly Father.

Even before it became evident through the call of President Israel A. Smith that I would serve in the general ministry of the church, there were events which took place pointing me in that direction. One of these, which is the basis for this testimony, took place early in my childhood as I stood at the foot of my father's bed when he was confined there in what proved to be a terminal illness.

My father was blind during the last several years of his life and, somewhat like Isaac in his relationship with Esau and Jacob, he had to depend on his other senses which had been developed to a sharp edge. He could distinguish persons by their voices with amazing accuracy. He could even identify people by the sound of their footsteps. So when he called me to come to his bedside, he knew when I arrived and queried, "Is that you, Wallace?" When I answered, he began to speak to me. He talked for a few minutes about family matters—how it would be up to me and my two brothers to carry on in a home without a father. He had no regrets. His had been a good life, and he was prepared to meet his God.

He was, however, concerned about the future leadership of the church and expressed this concern in words of advice and admonition. He had already provided for his immediate successor by designating his eldest son, Frederick M. Smith. He spoke to me more about what might be in store at a later date.

It is not my purpose here to be a chronicler of history, so let it suffice to say that Frederick M. Smith did become president of the church in 1915 and served in that capacity until his death in 1946. The pertinent part of this testimony is what happened as I stood at the foot of Father's bed.

Being only fourteen years old, I was not as aware of the significance of the occasion as I would have been at a more mature age. Nevertheless, the solemnity of having been called to appear before my earthly father as he prepared to meet his heavenly Father made a deep impression on my boyish mind. When he said, "Of you three younger boys, the burdens and responsibilities of the church will rest more heavily on your shoulders than upon either of the others," I was deeply impressed. I knew at that time that the Lord had a work for me to do. I did not know in what capacity I would be called upon to carry that responsibility, but I knew that sooner or later it would be my privilege to make a contribution to the Restoration movement.

The intervening years were full of struggles. Many trials and temptations were to be met and overcome. But in all this the hand of God ruled and overruled to my benefit. Now that he has given me the opportunity to serve as the leader of his church on earth, I take this occasion to thank him for the love and direction given me thus far in my ministry which has been under the influence of his Holy Spirit.

Many of us will find our faith being tested. We must be prepared to place our hand in the hand of God and to call on him for support and strength in times of need. Many problems of human relationship—man to man and man to God—have not been solved satisfactorily and will not be until we allow the pure, undefiled love exemplified by Jesus Christ to enter our hearts and take possession of us. Then, and only then, will we know God.

The Unopened Letters

By Elnora Watters

Four years ago last June I went to the doctor after a heart attack, praying that I would have no more. The doctor had been counseling me for some time to have surgery, but I didn't feel my condition was that bad.

After the doctor's examination he made a flat statement, "You have a year to live unless you have an operation now."

This is impossible, I thought. I'm alive now. Why should I let them open my heart?

For three months I prayed for guidance and a miracle to heal me without an operation. So many nights I lay awake, crying and thinking about my family. All I could think about was that I couldn't leave my children. They needed me. I had more attacks; they came often and were more severe.

Finally, while praying, I decided I could not go on like this. My husband and children were showing the strain, even though they didn't know the whole story. I arose from my knees, went into the kitchen, and wrote a letter to my husband and each of my children. I poured my heart out, asking them to have faith in God's decision. I sealed each letter, placed names on them, and put them into my dresser.

I awoke my husband and told him of my decision to have the surgery but said I wanted six months to teach the children everything I could concerning managing the house and getting along on their own if all did not go well. Also I wanted to make sure the hospital bills would be taken care of so that my husband would not have added bills.

He argued with me, but he was not aware that my condition was so bad. He always believed, however, that I would come out of surgery all right; I felt that I would not live through it.

It was hard to smile and act as if all were well while I was being torn apart inside. I was finding it difficult to go up and down steps, and I had a hard time walking across the street to a neighbor's house.

The children were good pupils—they learned fast. They became almost as good as I was at cooking and housework.

Now that I had placed myself in God's hands, I felt at peace until the six months were up. Then, for some reason, I lost my nerve and wanted to cancel the operation.

I had the elders of our church administer to me and I spent a month building my faith. Finally, I made arrangements at the hospital. But the operation was postponed another month because the hospital was overcrowded. On May 23, as we drove out of the driveway, I could see my four children standing on the porch, some holding on to the hands of a good friend.

They didn't cry—at least I did not see them—for they too had more faith than I. They knew I would come back, but I

88

still felt I would never see them again. I never looked back again as we drove to the hospital.

At the hospital, two elders from the Ann Arbor Branch came to see me and talk with me. One of them impressed me very much and said he would come back the next day. At that time I told him my fear of dying during the operation. He prayed with me and my faith in God increased. He told me he would be back before the operation or as soon as possible after. The next day I went to surgery with a prayer on my lips and tears in my eyes.

For a period of time everything was foggy. Each time I opened my eyes I saw either my husband, my sister, or the elder from Ann Arbor. Each time I saw the elder in the doorway I thought how nice it was of him to stay to make sure I would be all right. A few days later, after the worst was over, my husband told me that I had almost died.

Later the elder from Ann Arbor came to visit and I thanked him for coming to see me while I was in the recovery room. He was surprised. He told me he had not been there since he had not been able to get off work. God had used his form to show me that He was with me and would take care of me. I am not able to remember the name of the man nor have I seen him again, but I do know that God revealed himself to me through him. Twelve days after the operation I arrived home with love in my heart—for God, for my husband and children, and for life.

Several weeks later, I found the letters I had written to my family. At first I was going to throw them away; then I thought these might help the children and my husband to know my love for them, and God, so I gave them the letters to read.

Social Problems and Sainthood

By Gerald D. Evans

I have a testimony to share regarding God's love for the poor and the needy, the sick and the afflicted. I bear this testimony after many years of attempting to serve among the poor and the disadvantaged. As a social worker and counselor with a master's degree in social work, I have given most of my life to trying to help people. I have studied the problems of the poor, the causes contributing to such conditions, the needs of people in economic and social distress, and the various ways and means of assisting people.

While engaged in social work I have also endeavored to be a Christian and look at the needs of the poor through the spirit of Christ and the scriptures given by God. Continually I ask that Christ will walk with me in my stewardship and that God will send to me those whom I can help. I believe God has heard my prayers.

Before I decided to be a social worker an aged minister spoke to me much as a prophet of old and said, "You are going to bless many people in and out of the church." As a young person it was not possible for me to know how this could come about. At that time I was bashful and slow of speech and hesitated to attempt college. All I had "going for me" was a desire to prepare myself to serve God! Because of it, God touched my many weaknesses and made me strong for his purposes. Years later as a lay minister engaged in social work for the government I was introduced to a congregation to whom I was to preach as "He who has blessed many people in and out of the church." As these words were spoken I remembered the blessing given to me by the aged patriarch some twenty-five years previously.

In my testimony about God's love I must refer to what is in the scriptures and what is practiced. How to give financial assistance to the poor, the lame, the blind, and the widow and her children has been a controversial problem for centuries among Christians. The needy have been sent to the poorhouse and poor farm. Children have been taken from widowed or deserted mothers and placed with strangers or in institutions. The poor have been judged according to "worthiness" and denied a loaf of bread because of their failure to adhere to the giver's standards. Children have had to drop out of school to find employment because "welfare" did not give enough for necessities and held out only shame for those who received help. The poor have been given secondhand clothing and even rusty cans of food in Thanksgiving baskets. As I see it, society has attempted to minister to the poor in many ways contrary to the scriptures.

I find recorded in Holy Writ God's love and compassion for all his children—the sinner and the saint, the poor and the rich, the ill and the healthy. His instruction for the care of the needy and the disadvantaged differs much from the way they have been treated by society. The Book of Mormon plainly states that we are all beggars, and that we should "not suffer that the beggar putteth up his petition to you in vain, and turn him out to perish." Also, man should not say, "The man has brought upon himself his misery; therefore I will stay my hand, and will not give unto him my food, nor impart unto him my substance, that he may not suffer, for his punishments are just." Instead, the Book of Mormon teaches that we should administer "to their relief, both spiritually and temporally."

In the Doctrine and Covenants, one of the basic

principles within the spirit of stewardship is that surplus should be given to the bishop or storehouse "to administer unto those who have not, from time to time, that every man who has need may be amply supplied, and receive according to his wants." Contrary to many practices by welfare agencies, the Doctrine and Covenants also directs that the bishop, "should travel around about and among all the churches, searching after the poor, to administer to their wants." In Bible scriptures the story of the Good Samaritan as told by Christ illustrates how far one should go in helping the disadvantaged. Jesus made no statement as to denying anyone love but gave the Christian doctrine: "Love one another, as I have loved you. Greater love hath no man than this, that a may lay down his life for his friends."

In the method of ministry given by the church, I see the hand of God reaching out to the poor. Once a month in every church throughout the world church an offering for the needy is made. This money is administered to the relief of the poor by the bishop of the church and his representatives. Few churches within the Protestant world have provisions for the poor on such a regular basis.

As director of the Office of Social Ministries in the Center Stake of Zion, I have observed that those who come for financial help are usually not practicing church-taught stewardship which encourages the managing of possessions for God. Yet good stewards sometimes need help. Age, sickness, accidents, opportunities, environment, unemployment all affect us at times. I have also observed that many needy families have need for spiritual ministry as well as physical ministry. These families may have a variety of problems concerning health, rearing of children, debts, lack of work skills, absent father, etc. Therefore, there is a need for a variety of services to be given to those whom God loves. The giving of spiritual and temporal help to the needy was seen as a necessity by the people of God in Book of Mormon days. Within the last ten years the federal government has urged the states to include in their public welfare programs the giving of services along with public assistance checks. God has always been ahead! Although I may be interpreting the "spiritual" liberally, I also have observed that many of the poor of the church need to understand more about God and be committed more fully to Christ. This ministry is available through the various functions of the priesthood. God has provided a way for "spiritual" ministry as well as for "temporal" ministry.

Previously I stated that I asked God to send to me those whom I could help. I bear my testimony to the fact that God is active in ministering to the brokenhearted. On September 1, 1966, I became a full-time social worker-minister for the church. I was assigned to ministering to the needy of sixteen churches in Independence. In this newly created position I soon became aware that God would be sending people for special ministry.

One day my secretary came into my office with considerable concern and informed me that a woman had filled out an application for work through our employment agency, but because of the way she looked and acted I ought to talk with her. When the woman was seated in my office I saw a person who at first glance might look unattractive because of the condition of her hair, her face, and dress. But beyond that I saw the eyes of a person who was bewildered and miserable. She said nothing and I began asking questions cautiously. Finally I decided that she was missing loved ones. Guessing that she had a husband, I asked if her husband knew where she was. She shook her head. Then with a hope that she would say yes, I asked if I could call her husband. I was glad when she nodded her head affirmatively. When I reached her husband in a city nearby, I found a man full of anxiety and concern for the whereabouts of his wife. When he reached my office tears flowed down the woman's cheeks while she shyly smiled at him, and tears filled his eyes as he grasped her hand. One could easily see that she loved him, yet in my office was a woman running away from her children and husband.

Later, while counseling with her, I discovered that she had come to our agency for employment in spite of the advice by someone that the church would not help her. As I came to understand her problems from childhood to marriage to childbearing and learned that her suffering had started when she was a small child, I knew God had sent her to the Office of Social Ministries for help. The skills that God had given me were used in behalf of one of his beloved children. God's love was so great for this woman that tears come to my eyes when I recall the needs of this wonderful person. At the end of the first day of counseling I uttered a prayer for her that I will never forget. Christ went home with her and walked with her into her home.

Into the Latter Day Light

By Kasper Anholt

About thirty years ago at a district reunion, I listened to Floyd McDowell (who was then a member of the First Presidency of the church) preach a sermon. His sermon was about God and he referred to Him as "The central Source of light and power." He said that as he looked back on what had transpired in his life, it seemed that he was constantly directed by that unseen Power. It was as though he was walking down a long corridor. There were many doors leading from it, but he was always shown which one to open. He was positive that the Lord had directed him to the place that he held at that particular time. I too can say very much the same words. It seems that throughout my entire life there has been some unseen power that has directed me in my activities and led me to the present time.

Life for me as for many others has been a struggle from early childhood. My father and mother, who were both Norwegian, met and were married at Grafton, North Dakota. This was shortly after the turn of the century, and in 1903 a great deal of land was opened for homesteading in western Canada. It was then known as the District of Assiniboia, but is now part of the province of Saskatchewan. Homesteading lured my father and seventeen other young Norwegian couples to turn their faces northward and file on one hundred and sixty acres of land.

After they had filed on their land, it was necessary that they come back to Grafton where each worked in his own particular vocation to accumulate money for their new venture. My father was employed as a flour packer in a mill until the following spring when all the young men returned to their homesteads with the anticipation of building homes for their families who would come as soon as they were completed. What a cottage we called home! It was a sod house, yet to my parents it was as dear as any expensive home today. Even though ours was a sod house, it was nicely completed. The walls were about three feet thick, lined with lumber and papered, and there was a wooden floor. We also had a shingled roof with an attic, so the structure was warm and comfortable. It was in this home the following winter that I first saw the light of day. We were sixty miles from medical assistance so my father was both doctor and midwife. It is no wonder that many of the pioneer mothers died so young.

There were ten children born into our family. I was next to the oldest and this meant that as soon as I finished elementary school I had to leave home to work. Nearly all the money which I earned the first years was turned over to my father to help keep "the home fires burning."

For some reason or other it seemed to be the accepted thing in our family that I was to be a minister. At an early age I was nicknamed "The High Priest" which probably stemmed from the times when as children we played church. I would have all the others (the neighborhood children and my sisters and brothers) seated and we would sing old Norwegian hymns together. Then I would stand behind an improvised pulpit and "preach" to them. Perhaps because of this, when I was yet in my teens my parents arranged for me to attend a junior college sponsored by the Lutheran Church.

One of my studies at this school was theology. My marks in it were lower than in any of my other subjects. The reason for the low marks was that I answered examination questions according to my own interpretation of the scriptures. I felt that some of the answers which I had been given to certain questions were not according to the scriptures. It was then and there that I decided my "calling" to become a minister was only imagination. I did not doubt the church; rather I felt that if I had the aptitude to be a minister I would have understood.

I tried various occupations after that experience until I entered the grain business, where I worked for fifteen years. It was about this time that I met the girl who was later to become my wife. She was a member of my religious faith, one which we had both pretty well accepted.

When my father and mother had moved to Canada, my mother's sister and husband were in the same company. They filed on a homestead adjacent to ours so our homes were only about a quarter of a mile apart. They too had a large family of children whose ages matched ours. As children we played together a great deal and we thought almost as much of these cousins as we did our own brothers and sisters.

One of the children in my aunt's family was a girl named Nora who was seven years younger than I. At the age of twenty she died from pneumonia. Nora was a good girl. It was true that she had probably sowed a few "wild oats" and had missed some of her church obligations, but I was not prepared for the type of sermon that was preached at her funeral.

It was a sermon of condemnation which affected me so much that after we left the funeral I became very bitter and said most emphatically to my companion that if this was the type of God we worshiped I did not want any part of Him.

The feeling did not last too long, however. In my early childhood I had had experiences that had convinced me that there was a God, and in my study of him I was strongly impressed that he was a God of love. I felt that there was error in the condemnation which was heaped on Nora. Under the influence of the experience, I investigated the teachings of other denominations. I found many which agreed with the scriptures in one phase of doctrine but in others they seemed far removed from my interpretation. One thing I did notice, however, and that was that they all seemed to be in accord when it came to life after death. I kept on searching.

About a year later, the firm for which I was employed transferred me to a little town named Torquay in the southern part of the province of Saskatchewan. We were told that the people who lived immediately across the street from us were Mormons—a Mr. and Mrs. William Toovey. I was out in the yard working one evening when Mr. Toovey came across the street to talk to me. After our salutations and possibly some remarks about the weather, he asked me, "Do you do any reading?"

"Why, yes, I do a great deal of reading," I said.

"I have a book here," he remarked. "I wonder if you would care to read it?"

"Why, surely," I said, "I will be happy to," although I was more inquisitive than interested in what the Mormons might have to offer. He handed the book to me and I saw that the title was *Into the Latter Day Light,* by J. J. Cornish. William Toovey was a member of the Reorganized Church of Jesus Christ of Latter Day Saints and not a Mormon.

I can testify that from the very first chapter of the book I felt the presence of a Spirit that I had never experienced before. I never doubted anything that I read. I felt very strongly that if the church of Jesus Christ was on earth, then the same experiences should be available that were in the primitive church. What Brother Cornish wrote was very much in accord with this concept. I continued to study everything I could get my hands on. The same Spirit continued to stay with me, yet an entire year had elapsed before I decided I had waited long enough. On August 15, 1933, I was baptized late one evening after work in a little creek south of Torquay by the headlights of a car. After the baptism, I sat upon the running board while I received confirmation under the hands of the two elders.

Of course, there is much more to all of this than that which I have written. Even though I have had to make many explanations to my kin and friends (and sometimes have been reviled for my actions), yet if I had the opportunity all over again I would do the same thing. Over the years I have had many experiences that have convinced me that this work is God's work because it has revealed to me the love of a just and all-wise Father.

Putting My Trust in God

By Shirley Phillips

It was the Saturday before Thanksgiving and the warm day was refreshing after a cold seige. Our family went for a car ride which ended at a nearby lake. We went looking for pinecones to use as Christmas decorations and found a new foot trail with trees growing on both sides.

We had walked along the trail only about a hundred yards when suddenly I felt a sharp pain in my ankle. I jumped back and saw a small snake staring at me. Quickly my husband caught and killed it. We did not know if it was poisonous so we carried it with us as we hastened to the car. My husband helped me (for I was already unable to walk by myself) and the children walked ahead.

When we arrived back at the car a park ranger was standing nearby. My husband hurried to show him the snake. The ranger told us it was a very poisonous baby copperhead.

We loaded the children into the car and my husband drove rapidly to the nearest hospital. I tied the tourniquet with a hankie a little way above my ankle, thankful that this had not happened to one of the children.

Although it seemed like hours, it took us only a few minutes to reach the hospital. When we arrived my husband jumped out of the car and ran for assistance.

In the hospital emergency room, I had a slight pain but otherwise I felt fine. As a nurse I asked myself, *"When does a snake bite take effect? What does it do? I feel fine. I must not have gotten much venom; I'm not sick.* Shouldn't I be sick by now?" I asked aloud.

Yes, I was sick but did not feel it or know it. The doctors

could see my symptoms. They knew and worked with all the abilities men could muster, fighting against the effects of the venom. With a nursing background I knew more than most people would have known. I was blessed with peace and no fear.

While lying there, I asked my husband to call the leader of our congregational prayer circle. Then I asked him to call the chaplain at the Sanitarium to come and administer to me.

Since I was feeling so well, I did not want to remain as a patient. I wanted emergency treatment and then wished to be sent home or transferred to the Sanitarium. The doctor became concerned, for he could not get me to agree to admission.

Shortly after the prayer circle had started, however, I changed my mind. "I guess I don't have to be at the Sanitarium," I said to my husband. "It isn't necessary to have our family doctor. They know me here too. This doctor is good, and I trust him."

Before going to my room I had the children brought to me. I told them, "Snakebites can kill people. The doctors are doing all they can and so is Mommy. There is one stronger than the doctors—stronger than Mommy and Daddy. Do you know who I mean?" I asked. Glen answered, "God."

I replied, "That's right. God knows what is best and is in control. Remember this and if you become afraid, talk to him."

Then I left for my room. Shortly the chaplain from the Sanitarium arrived and administered to me. I was in serious condition for the next two days, but I was not afraid. I was at peace and trusting completely in God and my surroundings.

My condition improved slowly, but by Thanksgiving Day I was released from the hospital. My foot was still swollen but the doctor said I could recuperate at home. I had also lost some of the movement of my foot, but this was temporary. I would have to go to the hospital every day for therapy. All in all it was a wonderful Thanksgiving present. I have always enjoyed serving the Lord and I vowed I would use this experience also to serve.

Now lying here at home in bed, recuperating from the experience, I am writing my story. I am thankful to God for his unchangeability, for his unchangeable laws, and for knowledge. I know that when his laws are followed, the same result will occur each time.

I am thankful for my doctor who chose to learn the laws of healing and the nurses who chose to learn to assist. I am grateful for the hospital personnel who chose to use their time to serve mankind. I am thankful for the chaplain who chose to serve God in such way that God can continually work through him. I am thankful for my congregation and the prayer circle. I know man does not stand alone. I know we are our brother's keeper. I am thankful for these wonderful brothers.

God Still Guides

By Don Peterson

Fifty-three years ago my parents decided to move from the Omaha-Council Bluffs area to the rather primitive country of western Nebraska. There I spent my youth and grew into young manhood.

Both of my parents were members of the church; but since the nearest branch was about sixty miles from our country home and my parents felt we should be active in the

Lord's work, our church activity was centered in the community church of the neighboring town for a number of years. As a child and a young man, I regularly attended Sunday school, worship services, prayer meetings, and other activities of that church.

I graduated from high school and my parents provided the means for me to attend Graceland College. There I came to learn the true meaning of the Church of Jesus Christ and on one dusky, near-zero day, I was baptized into the church. I will long remember Elder D. Blair Jensen walking into the water of the Old North Pond, breaking the ice as he went, and my following him into the water to have my sins washed away.

Elder Roy A. Cheville confirmed my baptism in the Assembly Room of the old Graceland Administration Building. But the impressive services did not seem to make much change in my way of life.

After a year and a half of Graceland College, I returned to Nebraska to again attend the community church. I became a moderately successful businessman, married, and started a family.

During the next several years I was quite active in the community church, serving on the Board of Trustees or on some of the several commissions, teaching various classes, and serving as Sunday school superintendent. Despite the fact that my companion was an active member, and for all my activity, I never joined the church, although many ministers urged me to join. Somewhere in the back of my mind lingered the thought that God had led me into his church and that he had a definite place for me.

A common belief of the people of the various churches which I attended during these years was that I was a member, for many times at annual business meetings I would be nominated for eldership. I had to decline this office, for it was reserved to members of the church. My wife and I were always quite active in the youth activities. As an outgrowth of that association, I spoke in many different denominational services. Gradually, this expanded to lay services and sermons. I was filling pulpits during pastoral absences and vacations, and finally served for several months as a substitute pastor in a neighboring town.

Then circumstances came about which caused us to commute fifty miles to the Albin, Wyoming, branch of the Reorganized Church. On the first Sunday morning we walked into that little branch with its attendance of twenty people, I suddenly felt that I had come home! Almost immediately I knew that I would be called and would serve in the priesthood. Later, Pastor Ed P. Anderson confided to me that he had prayed long and earnestly for additional help, and as I walked into that service he was suddenly made aware that here was his help.

Within a very few months I was called to the office of priest and a year later to the office of elder. I have since experienced many wondrous and exhilarating experiences. I have been privileged to serve the church in many capacities.

My position as a management analyst with the U. S. Government has led me from Nebraska to Washington, Arizona, and Alaska. While in Arizona in 1963, I suffered what was thought to be a cerebral thrombosis attack and was bedfast for several weeks. I recovered from that attack and regained most of my bodily functions. Then about a year later, my wife and I drove to Fairbanks, Alaska, to accept another government position. Three months after our arrival, I was again stricken. This time the doctors determined that my malady was multiple sclerosis. Because of inadequate medical facilities, the government transferred me back to Tucson, Arizona, for treatment.

In both of these attacks, as I lay helpless and unable to

care for myself, I rededicated my life and services to Jesus Christ and his eternal purposes. In both instances my Creator heard my words, and I was granted the blessing of returning to almost normal physical ability. Recently, on a periodic physical recheck, my doctor said he never expected my present recovery—he never expected me to get out of bed again. Of his own volition, he said, "God must have a work for you to do!"

Now, once again, I am privileged to take up my work for God. I have come to know that God directs the lives and purposes of his children. As long as I am permitted to breathe his air, appreciate his world, it will be my desire to serve him in any capacity that he chooses for me.

My Conversion to Christianity

By Hideyuki Handa

In Japanese high school I studied Christianity as it related to world history, but I did not think about nor encounter Christ until I met my uncle. He was very friendly and I liked him, so I talked to him about many things that were on my mind—things which didn't have much to do with religion.

He seemed different than the ordinary Japanese, but I did not know why until my mother told me that he was a Christian. I began to wonder about what kind of man believes in God and what, specifically, Christians did. Since my uncle lived a long way from Tokyo, he visited us only once or twice a year. As a result I didn't have much time to talk to him about deep spiritual matters. Somehow, though, I felt there to be a beautiful quality in his personality and when in his presence I was always filled with peace. I respected my uncle and hoped I could be like him when I became a man.

Strangely enough, some time later, one of my friends invited me to attend the RLDS Church in Tokyo with him. I wondered where God was because my life had been completely secular. I was also very curious about the Christian environment, but curiosity itself doesn't last very long and my friend and I soon returned to our former pattern of life. After about three months, however, I felt some power pushing me back to church again. This time I was looking for God rather than people. I spoke frankly with the ministers about my life, asking for advice and counsel. They listened sincerely to what I said.

A few weeks later I had an interesting experience. I had passed the entrance examination for senior high school and was enjoying myself through clubs and student body activities. One day after school my group was responsible for cleaning the classroom. As usual, no one wanted to do it and I found myself alone—with all the other students gone. I looked around the room. It was dirty and dusty and I didn't want to clean it either. I knew I would feel silly cleaning the room by myself—and I didn't want to get dirty and embarrass myself in front of several girl students who would see me. Nevertheless, I picked up the dirty papers, swept the floor, and straightened the desks. I did what I was supposed to do, even though there was a great amount of work.

When I finished I was filled with peace and satisfaction. I decided to talk to the ministers about my experience. One of them said, "You met God there." I was surprised to learn that God was so near. I had thought that God must be far away—even beyond my conception. But he was so close! All of a sudden I was thankful for such a God, and was filled with a joy I hadn't known before. I felt alone and knew I needed some stronger power other than myself in order to become a better man. I thought about all the problems I had, and finally decided to depend upon God. Some months later I was encouraged to be baptized. I had been introduced to Christianity about four years before, but on June 1, 1969, I was baptized into Christ's church and began my new way of life.

Two months have passed as of this writing. Have I changed through baptism? I feel like the church is my home. Brotherly love, sincerity, compassion, and faith are there. Of course I sense God too. It is truly wonderful to make oneself humble and to be concerned about other people. I have found that God directs and leads my life. I love people because God loved me first. I want to help the church become more spiritual and friendly to the world.

God Leads Men to the Truth Today

By Harry Black

A reporter from a Warrington, England, newspaper became interested in the Restoration gospel after visiting the Warrington Branch for news items. His interest led to numerous discussions with various priesthood members and one evening during a missionary series he arranged with Seventies Black and Rowe to examine certain aspects of the Restoration message with a friend of his who was "well versed in the use of the scriptures." The friend was a retired doctor of dentistry, well known in the area as a lay preacher. "If there are flaws in your beliefs, Dr. Street will find them immediately," said the reporter.

The two seventies agreed to time and place and a few

days later made their call. As they arrived at the pensioner flat of Dr. Street an elderly woman was leaving. Dr. Street introduced her as a neighbor and friend. No mention was made to her of the vocations of the visiting ministers, but her interest—especially her gaze—was affixed almost to the point of embarrassment.

The two men entered the flat and the discussion of gospel principles and scriptural references progressed under a delightful spirit of mutual interest and respect. Finally Dr. Street said he could accept the message of the church quite readily on the basis of scriptural knowledge, but he wondered about the Restoration claim of divine revelation being resident within specialized priesthood.

"I'll pray about the matter," he promised. "Only a personal testimony, if such be possible, can prove your words."

After arranging to return the next day with more literature, the seventies left the flat. The elderly neighbor woman was standing at her apartment door, gazing intently at them. She smiled in acknowledgment as they passed.

On the following day when they returned to continue their discussion Dr. Street greeted them with these words, "Yesterday I welcomed you as guests; today I call you brothers. I have received evidence of your divine priesthood authority and wish to become a member of your church." He then told how, after their leaving, the neighbor woman had knocked on his door and had greeted him with these words: "Dr. Street, I don't know who those men were, but a power I have never known before told me that they were sent from God to instruct you."

After his baptism, Brother Street never failed to bear witness of God's guiding hand to those who search after righteousness. By the same divine power which bore witness of the truth through Elders Rowe and Black, Dr. Street himself was called to the office of priest. He labored diligently until God called his aged body home.

As the love of God answered an old man's plea for the truth it touched the heart of his neighbor who also became a member of the church.

I Put God to the Test

By Peter Taylor

My earliest recollection of attending church was in a little old Church of England church in the seaside resort of Bondi in Sydney, Australia. I was six years old, dressed in a choir robe with a stiff, starched collar, singing in an anniversary service. It was a hot humid day and the church was packed to capacity; I well remember listening to the waves crashing on the beach (which was not more than half a mile away) and wishing I was there swimming with the holiday crowds. Like most small boys, I looked for the time when I would be old enough not to have to attend.

We moved from Bondi to one of the western suburbs of Sydney, and almost immediately I left junior school to attend high school. Being the youngest of three brothers, my parents decided that I should go to a private school and for the next five years I attended a strict Catholic college. I remember vividly the various classes of instruction. Since I was non-Catholic, I did not have to take the Basic Religion subject. While this study was conducted, I caught up on my homework. I often listened to the discussions that went on and probably, for the first time, I was made aware of man's relationship to God—so much so that I even prayed the way that was suggested, fasted, and went to confession; but in all this I found no God, no answer to prayer, or anything else. I became a nonbeliever.

I loved sports, especially football; and after leaving school to go to work as a mechanical fitter, I played quite a deal of football for the district in which I lived. During this period, I met some young people with whom I worked who belonged to a Church of Christ young people's group. I was invited to attend and it wasn't too long before they asked me to join the church football club. The fellowship of these young people was wonderful and it was through them that I came to know a Mr. and Mrs. Morris who had three daughters and two sons. Their younger son, Ern, and I became firm friends and for many years we did everything together. I joined the Church of Christ by baptism, but I still felt no different religiously than when I was attending college. I joined because I wanted to belong to the group.

It wasn't too hard to leave when Ern's brother-in-law asked us to play football with the Reorganized Church of Jesus Christ of Latter Day Saints—one church was the same as another, as long as we had a good time and plenty of football. It was necessary to attend church one Sunday per month in order to qualify for membership in the team, but that was easy. I listened each time I attended, and once again came that challenge to put my trust in God and believe.

During my association with the football team, I met and married a girl who was a staunch member of this new church. Just prior to our marriage (more to gain favor with my fiancée than anything), I was baptized into the church, but still I had no real conviction about God.

At twenty-three years of age my vocation in life had altered and I was now responsible for a business controlling sales stock and figures and was in charge of six people. The new responsibility was a worry to me and through it all was this continual nagging question about God. I studied the scriptures, I prayed, and I fasted. But to no avail. I was greatly disturbed and felt that my searchings were fruitless; again I turned my back on God. It just seemed that I could receive no answer or response and I was completely and utterly disillusioned. Attending church was a waste of time and I had a lot of "living" to do.

Through the appeal of my wife, I went to one more service, Communion, and resolved that if I had no answer to my problem, then I would give it all away. To my astonishment and yet my delight, the pastor spoke to me by the gift of the Spirit and revealed to me three things:

1. God was vitally concerned with all men and yet was personally interested in me.
2. If I answered his call, the problems associated with my vocation would be solved and I would be helped to accept the responsibilities entrusted to me.
3. If I believed and trusted in him for help, he had a work for me to do in the priesthood and I would never again doubt his existence in his church.

I glowed from within for about two weeks. I felt very close to God while feeling very inadequate, but I promised to obey his will. From that day to this, I have never doubted his existence or his purpose for man. It has been my privilege to serve in the church as an elder for ten years in many different positions, and my growing conviction is that God lives in the lives of men and women as they endeavor to obey his commandments. As a loving heavenly Father, he is vitally concerned with the individual needs and strivings of his children.

Why don't you put God to the test?

"Ask and it shall be given you; seek, and ye shall find; knock and it shall be opened unto you."

Commitment to the Practical

By Courtney L. Hunter

Twenty years ago I was motivated to a decision of baptism because I had deep personal problems that were too big for me to handle by myself. If I were not a member today, I think I would choose alignment with the Church of Jesus Christ because of its commitment to a practical, workable ideal of brotherhood for all mankind.

Of course, at the time of my baptism I subscribed to the establishment of Zion, but it was a hazy, nebulous kind of understanding that took a back seat to the more pressing demands of my personal problems. I needed more than anything at that time a satisfying personal relationship with God. I needed the assurance that he cared for *me* personally. Even more basic, I needed to know that he existed.

And so I read the history of the church and some of the Book of Mormon (and balked somewhat at the fantastic story of Joseph Smith and the golden plates), and I began to attend a church school class regularly. As I moved closer to a decision of baptism (in my case, so aptly put by Kierkegaard as the "leap of faith"), I think I was more influenced by the graceful impact on my life of kind, concerned, interested Saints than answers to my intellectual curiosity. And too, I was beleaguered by a determined missionary whose broad, simple faith in God intrigued me.

The strangest part about my years of membership in the church is that even today I cannot handle my problems alone. Therein lies a challenging paradox. By accepting the fact that I can never handle my own problems, I have found

111

the secret and key to their solution—I can do nothing without God.

Having discovered the great promise that is resident in Jesus' words: "If ye have faith as a grain of mustard seed...," I have moved beyond concern for my own moments of despair. For some years now I have been more interested in what both church and community members can do to help ease the miserable plight of others.

I like working within the organized structure of the church. There are people like me, as I was twenty years ago, who need my help to come to grips with their personal problems. There are others who challenge my thinking about the brotherhood of man. Yes, I can and do find both kinds of people outside the church, but there is something else. This something has to do with the symbolic power of the ordinances of baptism and confirmation by the laying on of hands.

People are most psychologically healthy when they have transferred their latent goals and ambitions into physical and material symbols. For example, I love my children. Not only do I give verbal expression to this feeling but I also perform acts of love that demonstrate my feeling. Notwithstanding the benefit to my children, the benefit to me is tenfold. I have put myself on record, and when I am successful in measuring up to that record the pleasure, satisfaction, and sense of well-being is infinite.

Thus, I look at baptism and confirmation as important symbolic ordinances that assist me in achieving my innermost desire—to be of worth to others. By publicly committing myself to the ideals of Christian brotherhood I have taken the first necessary step toward the accomplishment of my goal.

Something Was Missing

By Florence E. Berry

When I was a child, I felt that my parents were trying to "drive" me into religion. But I was stubborn and resisted. I can remember sitting through church services feeling very bored and wishing that the speaker would hurry up. Prayer meeting was especially dull, for there was no piano music and everything was more quiet than on Sundays.

As I grew old enough to assert myself, I firmly rebelled against my parents' insistence that I attend church. I could see nothing for me there and it wasn't long before I began to partake of the worldly things so much that my parents were constantly worried about where I was, who I was with, and what I was doing. I was in trouble more times than I care to remember, but my parents were always there, ready to give me another chance to pull myself together.

I finally married a man whom I had known only ten days. My brother and father were certain that it would not last, for I had never carried out anything that I started. I suppose the love my husband had for me and the determination I had that our marriage would work pulled us through the first years of marriage. I knew also that if the marriage didn't work I would probably deteriorate to a greater degree—and end up on the "scrap pile of humanity." This was one thing I did not want to have happen to me.

It was not long before children were included in our family. By the time we were expecting number four, I suddenly realized that I had nothing of real value to give to them. What I had to teach them amounted to almost nothing.

Gradually I began to think again of the things which I had been taught in church and how important they were.

It was not long until I began taking my children to church. I learned also the important things that had been missing in my life. Soon my husband joined and we became a family united in the church. Our progress has been slow and at times very discouraging, but we have "grown up" spiritually.

Now I realize how much trouble my parents went through in the years of my adolescence. I am most grateful for the loyalty they gave me. I am thankful that God gave them strength to pray for my deliverance, for I am sure that without His help, I would have been lost long ago.

I wish to be able to shoulder the responsibility that is mine and give my all for the cause of Jesus Christ and the church. I want to be among those who can say that they are the children of God at the last day.

Inner Evidence

By Hendrik Compier

I am one of those individuals to whom the testimony of the Book of Mormon has not come in a miraculous way. I have not had the privilege of seeing the ruins and archaeological remains of South America, Central America, and Mexico which for many are additional evidences that strengthen their convictions concerning the truth of the book. Neither am I one of those who has had an unusual interest in the story of the American Indian—his background, history, folklore, and legends. Besides this, because of my Dutch background, I have never been much of a student of American history and the origin of peoples inhabiting the American continent.

My testimony of the Book of Mormon, then, does not necessarily rest on any of the usual evidences. I do admit to the value of these additional evidences and also that I gained interest in these areas of study after having become more thoroughly acquainted with the book. For me the testimony of the Book of Mormon lies in the book itself.

I have come to appreciate the Book of Mormon first of all because of its plainness, honesty, simplicity, directness, boldness, and unapologizing approach. Nephi, one of the early writers from the book, promised to write "according to the plainness which hath been with me from the time that I came out from Jerusalem with my father." In other places he speaks of the "plainness of the gospel" (I Nephi 3:165) when he speaks about the preservation of the records of the Jews. He also speaks of the "plainness which is in the Lamb of God" (I Nephi 3:174) in his explanation that many shall stumble because of plain and precious things being taken from the gospel of the lamb. (Apparently this means the recordings of the Bible which seem to have lost many of their essentials and some which may have been left out through translation.) Nephi also said: "My soul delighteth in plainness unto my people, that they may learn." Besides Nephi other writers such as Jacob, Enos, and Alma referred specifically to this plainness and others again seemed to discipline themselves to being clear without "beating around the bushes." It is refreshing to read straightforward language.

The Book of Mormon helps explain many things which are touched upon in the Bible, but which are not always clear, concerning life according to God's plan. I certainly do not view the book as a substitute for the Bible; neither do I like to refer to it as a "second Bible." Many times those who are not members of the Reorganized Church of Jesus Christ of Latter Day Saints have stated that Latter Day Saints use a "second Bible." The Bible speaks for itself and certainly its greatness can never be fathomed. Nevertheless the Book of Mormon can be seen in many ways as a commentary upon the Bible, as well as a book of scripture entitled to its own name. It stands *with* the Bible and serves as a tremendous source book of inspiration and insight into the plan of God for us today, as well as for those who have gone before. Many doctrines of the gospel of Jesus Christ such as baptism, repentance, faith, authority of priesthood, etc., are made very clear in the Book of Mormon. In no way does it contradict the Bible, but gives additional insights. Alma's marvelous sermon on faith as found in the sixteenth chapter of the book by his name is a good illustration of additional insight into the nature of dynamic, active, working faith. Moroni's instructions on baptism adequately explain why baptism before one reaches a responsible age is not appropriate. Throughout the book the theme of repentance is stated with many clear examples of what can happen when man repents—and also, on the contrary, what happens when man continues to rebel against God.

I appreciate the Book of Mormon because it appears to be a "fresh" account. By this I mean that it has not gone through many translations. It has not existed as long as the Bible. It has the additional advantage of "having been translated by divine command." All this is by no means a plea for a view of perfection for the book. Man would be most out of touch with reality to consider any work with which his hands are connected as being perfect. In fact, Mormon himself seems to warn of this in a preface: "And now if there are faults, they are the mistakes of men; wherefore, condemn not the things of God, that ye may be found spotless at the judgment seat of Christ." This is an open admittance to the possibility of error.

Again, compared to the Bible, we can see great advantages in what I have called "freshness." It is most obvious that the Bible is not an infallible book either. A comparison of different translations of the Bible and the many different shades of meaning which have evolved indicates that errors have crept in because of faulty translations. Added also are the many errors which have crept in through copying throughout the ages and those which have appeared because someone wanted the Bible to represent a particular trend of thought, philosophy, or theology. It is surprising that there is as much uniformity in the different versions, editions, and copies of the Bible as there is. That there would be opposition to such a book as the Book of Mormon is made clear in the book itself. Nephi foretells in II Nephi 12:45 that people will say in our day: "A bible, a bible, we have got a bible, and there can not be any more bible."

The Book of Mormon deals with people just as they are—in many ways like people today. Human nature is much the same throughout all time. Often, in reading modern works of literature, we miss the "human touch," that essence of humanity which all ages have in common. This is not the case with the Book of Mormon. Here are people just as they are—with vices, jealousies, pride and anger, and much childish behavior. The writers do not try to cover up for their people. Humanness is plainly exposed. The preservers of the records often described themselves as being "poor in writings" (II Nephi 15:1).

I appreciate the Book of Mormon because it speaks clearly to our times. Its message is full of meaning and intent for our day. Time and again we read that the records from which the book came were preserved in order that they might be brought forth in our time. The prophets of the Book of Mormon were aware that what they said and did would have meaning particularly in the day when the book would be published and used as a testimony to the peoples of the earth. The book deals prophetically with much material which is characteristic of our day and time. It deals with the issues of race relations, war and peace, morals and the weakening of morality in our day. It is concerned with the denying of Christ and the power of God—so typical of our day even to the denial of the very existence of God and Christ. It speaks of people who will say in our day that they have no need of God, that they have "come of age" and can take care of things themselves. It is full of descriptions of our modern age and its manifold problems in relation to God. Even the hesitancy to accept the book in the latter days was seen by the Book of Mormon writers. Moroni's invitation in the tenth chapter of the book by his name (the last book of the Book of Mormon) is a sensing of this need for many in our day, and the challenge is before us to "ask God with a sincere heart, with real intent."

My appreciation of the Book of Mormon finds its climax in the testimony of the Christ which has increased because of the book. Certainly it is a witness of Jesus Christ. This is its central theme and message and it was written to this end. As we observe the Book of Mormon writers bearing witness of this Jesus Christ (his full name is mentioned very frequently even at the first) whose birth, life, suffering, crucifixion, and resurrection were foretold to those who lived before his actual coming upon the earth, our hearts are warmed. With insight and clarity and by the power of God himself they describe his suffering for all mankind, the meaning of his atonement, and his plan of redemption for all. What a picture of love, concern, true fatherhood, sacrifice, hope, and salvation!

During my assignment in the Netherlands Mission, the mission leadership decided to base the theme of our Easter

Camp (the reunion for the Saints in the Netherlands) on the Book of Mormon. We had a marvelously unifying experience as we centered our thoughts on its meaning, its coming forth, its message as related to the Bible, its significance for us today, and its enriching influence in the life of the church.

I was selected to bring the message to the campers on Easter Sunday morning. My concern for this sermon was a matter of weeks. I had read, I had made many notes. In a way it might be said that I was prepared, yet in many respects I was not. I knew I needed more than I could offer in my own strength. As I studied and prayed I felt led to read again the account of the appearance of the Christ in America as found in Nephi:

"And it came to pass that he stretched forth his hand and spake unto the people, saying, Behold I am Jesus Christ, of whom the prophets testified should come into the world:

"And behold I am the light and the life of the world, and I have drunk out of that bitter cup which the Father hath given me, and have glorified the Father in taking upon me the sins of the world, in the which I have suffered the will of the Father in all things, from the beginning.

"And it came to pass that when Jesus had spoken these words, the whole multitude fell to the earth, for they remembered that it had been prophesied among them that Christ should show himself unto them after his ascension into heaven.

"And it came to pass that the Lord spake unto them, saying, Arise and come forth unto me, that ye may thrust your hands into my side, and also that ye may feel the prints of the nails in my hands, and in my feet, that ye may know that I am the God of Israel, and have been slain for the sins of the world."—III Nephi 5:11-14.

I found myself enveloped in the Spirit of God, to the point where I cried out, "Lord, it is enough; this is the testimony of the Book of Mormon I was seeking." I sensed more than ever before the love and deep concern of God and Christ for all creatures regardless of where they are. My prayer had been answered, and I entered the pulpit that Easter morning with concern but with confidence that the Lord would use me to speak of his love and hold before his people his light and his life—the life of the resurrected Christ unto their salvation.

The Pure Love of Christ

By Georg Sofke

Through God we are given the power to love our enemies.

I have often noticed when conversing with other Christians about the doctrine of Christ that they will usually agree with me on most points. But rarely do they agree when I come to the point made in Matthew (5:46), "But I say unto you, love your enemies, bless them that curse you and despitefully use you."

I do not understand why such a large number of people feel this commandment need not be kept. It is still harder for me to understand why members of my own church must be counted among this number. Biased opinion could be a reason, but surely it isn't the only one.

I no longer make snap judgments. When I finally make a decision it is a firm one and I abide by it. I have meditated often on Matthew's scripture and have concluded that with God's help it is possible to keep this commandment. With this framework let me try to describe an experience I had as a boy.

In 1942, when we were in the third year of World War II, a young Polish couple moved into the same house in which we lived. At that time I was only eleven years old. Both husband and wife worked, so I rarely saw them. About a year later, the young wife had her first baby. Since my mother was also employed and I was always alone after school, I tried to spend my time with this young couple whenever they were home. We became good friends. When the child was about a year old it suddenly became sick and died. My mother could not get off work to go, but I went to the funeral which was held one morning before school. On the way to the church I met my teacher, a former major in the army and a member of the Nazi Party.

Later, at school, he made an example of me before the whole class. He pointed to me and said, "Look at Sofke there. He calls himself a German. I don't suppose he's noticed we are in the fifth year of the war, for it seems he attends the funeral services of his enemies."

I knew only too well that we were in the war, for I had already lost my oldest brother in the senseless endeavor. But I had learned the commandment of the Lord, "Love your enemies," and in my home the word of God was held in greatest esteem.

I will admit it isn't always simple to keep this commandment. However, with God's help it is possible. I know now that during World War II there were Saints in England, Holland, U.S.A., and other places who kept this commandment. And I know brethren now who are willing to keep the commandment whether in Vietnam or somewhere else.

In order to build Zion, we can't keep just those

commandments that are easy to keep. Even young Nephi in the Book of Mormon (1:65) knew that the Lord does not give his children a commandment without giving them that which they will need in order to obey it. When we are willing to give our best, then the Lord will enable us through his power to become a light to the world of the future.

An Apostle's Testimony

By Clifford A. Cole

It isn't easy for most people to talk about God. For that matter we generally find it difficult to talk seriously about any of the deepest, most gripping experiences of life. These are the issues that hit us the hardest because they deal with things that really make a difference. Some of these matters are personal, and we do not want to open them to the prying eyes of those who do not share our feelings about them. Often we fear disclosing our innermost attitudes, lest others tread irreverently over sensitive areas of our hearts. We may very often allow some of the convictions which once seemed sacred to us to slip away because, having buried them in our hearts we have hidden them from ourselves and have allowed the shallow and the cynical to blur the value which we once placed upon them. Many a person has found this true as he has begun to associate with people who do not share his values and patterns of life. The young person who enters military service or goes to college may find himself so overwhelmed by associates who ridicule what he has considered sacred that he buries it and finds himself trying to be one of the group in thought and actions. But this is not a problem reserved to youth. Adults also find the attitudes of those at the factory or the office seeping into their lives like fog silently pouring in through the cracks and crevices of a house.

It is in the face of this problem that many persons have found it good to cultivate companionship with those who share their values and who are pleased to talk about sacred things. In the church we sometimes call this sharing one's testimony. The word "testimony" may sound sanctimonious and therefore not appeal to many people. Call it what you will, it designates an activity in which every person ought to engage if he really wants to stand for something. Reaching down into the depths of one's heart and bringing again into the light those things which are precious strengthens the convictions developed when one was at his best. Furthermore, it is just such shared experience that helps to strengthen others. Strangely enough when one is in a group which seems to overwhelm him with the cynical, shallow, or even an immoral atmosphere, he will find that a testimony relative to the deeper meanings in his own life will inspire others to disclose the fact that they also have values and convictions which they have kept hidden because they have drifted away from previously held patterns or have been too timid to express thoughts which might be ridiculed.

When one probes for deeper meanings he inevitably finds himself in the midst of the sacred. He also is confronted by the ultimates of his being. He deals with the questions of life's purpose and meaning either in regard to his own life or the lives of his children and loved ones. He stands in the presence of death and birth and love. He must see himself in relationship to others and eventually to God. Many, of course, will quickly say, "I don't know whether or not there is any meaning or purpose to life. I don't know that there is a God." I wouldn't argue this point too much; I am sure the answer depends upon what kind of proof one is willing to accept. There are very few things one can prove beyond a doubt, and many things in life which once seemed tightly nailed down have now been pried loose.

However, in the midst of such a fluid, shifting world, there are some things that good men through experience still find to be stable. These values are like stars in the heavens to guide one across the vastness of the rolling, moving seas. Honesty, compassion for others, responsibility to one's family and the society in which one lives—these and other virtues like them are not outdated. One can hardly avoid the conclusion that some ways lead to happier, more meaningful lives. When we begin to probe these values in depth we are confronted by the question of purpose and meaning in the universe. Such purpose brings us back to the source of all that is, and this is God. This creative Source can be warm and personal.

When I am at my best I sense not only power and force at work within the universe but also the presence of Personality. I sense that I am not alone in the midst of energy actively at work, but I am loved so that I can no longer speak of this presence as "it." I must say I am in the presence of "Him."

It is a serious thing for a person to say, "I believe in God"; one does not say such a thing lightly. On the other hand, it is just as serious to say, "I do not believe in God." No one can respect the flippant person who, ridiculing the idea of God, cites what seem to him obvious evidences of error in the faith of others without paying the price to dig deeply enough to discover less obvious answers.

I am convinced that God has at one time or another touched the lives of most of us in ways which, for that moment, gave us assurance of a divine Presence. Sometimes these experiences relate to matters that are personal and do not seem to be of importance to anyone other than the person involved. On the other hand, they are often profound experiences affecting movements of historical significance. For instance, I witnessed the prayer of a distraught man searching for his lost keys answered immediately; he lifted his head and said, "I know exactly where I will find those keys." This was knowledge accompanied by the awareness of a concerned Presence. On the other hand, I have felt the impulsion of an inner Presence directing me to pray for a whole community in great need, and have seen that prayer answered as I was directed to pray, by what I fully believe to be the power of God. There is a great difference in the importance of these two experiences as far as human values are concerned, but I am reminded that God can be found in the so-called insignificant "flower in the crannied wall" as well as in crucial moments when the destiny of nations hangs in the balance.

God has not left himself without evidences for those who seek him. Many years ago I was sitting in a college physics class. The discussion turned to certain natural phenomena which science had helped us understand but which once were explained only by saying that they were the acts of God. As we talked, one of the students said, "Don't you really think the day will come when all the things we now call supernatural will be explained so that we won't need to attribute them to God?" The instructor, whom I had always considered to be a man of cold analytical science and not a man of religion, said in thoughtful response, "No I don't think so." Then he related this experience which I shall quote as nearly as memory will allow. Said the instructor, "I was awakened in the night after having an experience during my sleep in which I was visited by the presence of my mother. She told me that she had just died and had some things she wanted me to know before she passed on. Then she bade me good-bye. I awoke in great emotional distress and looked at my alarm clock. It was three o'clock. The experience was so real and so vivid that I could not get it off my mind nor go back to sleep. In the morning a telegram was delivered telling me that my mother had passed away at three o'clock that night."

The class was sobered and again realized, in the testimony of this honest man, that we do not live merely in a mechanical universe but in the presence of Personality which has personal concern for each of us.

There are those who want to put the problem in such a way as to test God. They say if the experience is miraculous and not explainable by any natural phenomena it is of God. This makes it appear that God is not involved in natural law or creation through natural processes. For the person of godly faith there can be no distinction between the unexplainable and that which we understand. I do not love my wife the less because I understand her more as the years go by—nor does she become less real. The gifts of her love become more meaningful and appreciated. So it is with our love for God and our sense of his presence. He is in all of life. All power and all being rest in him. There are no benefits which we receive that are not of his creation.

It is good to acknowledge the holiness and love of God and to speak of those experiences with him which have blessed and enriched our lives. The wise sharing of those good things which are deepest and which direct attention to the ultimates in life is a source for renewing our own faith and enlarging the faith of others. In turn, when they share with us those matters of deepest value and concern to them, we are blessed by it. It is for this reason that members of the church feel it is a privilege to meet together in prayer and testimony services and enjoy opportunities for more sustained association such as those at week-long reunions, camps, and conferences where in the company of others who share their values they can be most truly themselves. It is a joy to be among people who understand.

One God — One Mind

By Saku Sekine

Never before was I so strongly convinced of "One God—One Mind" as when I participated in the Oiso Retreat as a member of the team of Orient field missionettes. It certainly was a mountaintop experience. As we worshiped together, prayed, studied, and fellowshiped, our spiritual tie was strengthened. Once again we were reassured that those who are in the faith are found in one fellowship.

The retreat centered around two themes—"Life of Spiritual Power" and "Improvement of Human Relationships." We learned from this experience that the only source of harmony and comfort to our troubled souls is faith in one God. We were reminded of the importance and necessity of constantly placing our utmost trust in the One who is extending his guiding hand—challenging us to move Zionward.

As we strolled the nearby seashore we discovered an inexpressible peace of mind and calmness of soul. Our footprints were soon washed away by the incoming waves, but the emotional impact of this experience will never be erased. It will remain in the heart of each of us as a constant reminder of an ever growing sisterhood in Christ in whose footsteps we are seeking to follow.

I brought home with me three rather pretty pebbles gathered along the beach. As I occasionally move them around in my hand I can still hear the conversation shared among us. Pebbles on the beach are continuously being smoothed and made round by the ceaseless flow of the waves. so, in like manner, our lives are being matured by the waves of criticism, sorrow, and trouble. Yes, if we are to know the love of God we must overcome the waves of temptation in this world. Fears and uncertainties of our earthly life must be conquered by our becoming God-fearing children.

If we are truly sons and daughters of God, professing the same heavenly Father, how can it be that hatred and misunderstanding exist among us?

If we are truly brothers and sisters in Christian love, then we must be genuinely concerned with each other's welfare. What we do and say to one another must be based on mutual respect and understanding. Only as we incorporate this faith in our daily lives can we say, "We, too, believe in the same God."

I know the Oiso experience will forever sustain my life of witnessing for Christ—enabling me to go and see beyond the horizon. I know I will be greatly strengthened and assured if I uphold this renewed conviction in my soul. We are one in Him.

Preserved for a Purpose

By Joseph Henry Lewis

In the year 1952 I became so dangerously ill that I was rushed to the Royal Hospital at Wolverhampton, in a dying condition. It was doubted that I would last the night. My parents were filled with anguish, but my life was spared—a remarkable fact which I have always been convinced was due, in addition to the skill of the medical profession, to the prayers of my family, my friends, and my church. At that time I was a Methodist preacher. I have subsequently felt that my life was preserved by God for some definite purpose, but was never quite aware of the nature of that purpose.

In 1961 I lost the job I had held with an engineering firm in Birmingham for twenty years. I secured a post with a larger firm almost immediately. The events which led me to this new place of employment were of such remarkable coincidence that I find it more feasible to believe that the hand of God was at work.

At my new place of employment there existed a small but well established Christian fellowship which met each Wednesday at lunchtime. I knew about it but never joined. I was at this firm (Joseph Lucas Ltd.) for six years before I felt the urge to join in the fellowship of the L.C.F.

About this time a young RLDS self-sustaining minister was having difficulty at his place of employment. Due to another surprising series of events he came eventually to the firm where I was employed. Late in the year of 1967 I met him for the first time—at the Lucas Christian Fellowship. Quite gradually I formed a very casual sort of acquaintance. The circumstances which had led each of us to the firm were so remarkable that the only reasonable explanation was the sheer providence of God at work, though at the time we did not know this.

I saw him occasionally at the L.C.F. and had the usual friendly exchanges as I did with the others. However, I became aware of a marked difference in this young minister. He showed true dedication and I discerned a depth of spirituality which caught my attention. One day he was absent from the fellowship. I was so uneasy about his absence that I felt impelled to write to him—although I didn't know him very well. I did not realize that in doing this I triggered a course of events which were to alter the whole tenor of my life.

The time came for him to give an address to the fellowship. It took the form of a very moving personal testimony which impressed me tremendously. I had never heard a testimony like it before.

Gradually I warmed to this very dedicated young man. If he saw me in the toolroom where I worked, his hand would go up in greeting. Frequently he would address me as "brother" or say, "God bless you." He was not afraid to quietly say grace before a meal. I was truly impressed with his genuine Christian bearing, his courtesy, his concern for people, and his love for his Lord and his church.

The acquaintance continued, the conversations lengthened, and the various aspects of his testimony were expounded. My questions increased and we talked at lunchtime. I had never met anyone quite like him before. His church was his passion.

The acquaintance developed into friendship and my interest in his church was thoroughly aroused. He shared the Book of Mormon, the Doctrine and Covenants, and, every month the *Restoration Witness.* No aspect of the church was neglected as far as he was concerned. He visited me at my home and won the loving esteem of my aged father. I had never had a friend like this before. The church was constantly on his lips, yet was never awkwardly or obtrusively advocated.

It is a belief of mine that one can judge the spiritual quality of a church by the nature of the hymns it sings. I examined the hymnal used by Reorganized Latter Day Saints and discovered that about two hundred of the great hymns of christendom and about twenty-four of Charles Wesley's were contained in it. This seemed to confirm the rightness of the church's theology in a particular way to my "Methodist" mind. It satisfied me in a way I needed satisfaction. During 1968 I began to visit his church and the weekly prayer services. They were just what I had been needing for a long time.

One evening in October I came home from work with a feeling of acute depression, for I had not had a good day. I had seen my friend briefly, and he said that he had some pastoral visits to make. During the evening I was deeply troubled, and in tears I called on God to help me. After a while I engaged myself with some task in hand. While making a telephone call, I heard the outer door open. In a moment a familiar face peeped around the door at me. It was he.

"Whatever brings you here tonight?" I said. "I thought you had some visiting to do."

"Yes," he replied, "I did, but when I got home tonight something told me I had to come here. I felt impelled to come, and I always obey my impulses. So here I am."

I was dumbfounded! "Well," I gasped, "you don't know how right you are. You little know how I needed you. Your coming here at this moment is a marvel—it's a *miracle!* And if you always obey the Holy Spirit like that—my word—you *are* a minister." When he left that night I was a new person.

A week later he was stricken with an ailment. I saw him in his office in great pain and discomfort. Sometime later in the day I received a call informing me that he had met with a motor accident on his way to the doctor's. His car had been hit by another at a crossroads and badly damaged. He was not injured, but was shaken. I contacted him as soon as possible by phone and he informed me that the doctor said he was "a hospital case," needing special treatment. "How do you feel?" I asked. "Harry," he replied, "I don't know what I'm going to do. I'm at my wit's end."

The moment I was free I went to him. He was in a very nervous and distressed state as a result of the car accident. He said that he had an appointment for an administration at the church but was in no state to go. I asked the elders to come to his home. Within minutes the pastor and another elder came. This was my first experience with administration, and to my surprise one of them asked me to lead in prayer. I was deeply moved by the honor of participating in an ordinance I had never witnessed before. I prayed briefly for the power of the Holy Spirit to come upon us. The pastor anointed the head of my friend with oil and offered a short prayer. The other man then offered a most wonderful and powerful prayer for the pain and sickness to be removed from my friend. I was deeply impressed by the complete rightness of it all. It was so true and so near to the teachings of the New Testament.

For several weeks preceding Christmas I was plagued with unusual pains which moved at times from my ankle to my hip. I found it difficult to work properly as I couldn't stand in one position. A doctor could not locate the trouble. With little or no treatment the pain was proving to be a distinct handicap. This so worried my friend that he came to me and said, "Harry, don't you think you ought to have administration for that leg?"

"Oh, I don't know," I replied. "I've never had an administration and besides I'm not a member of the restored church."

"That doesn't matter," he said. "Anyway I want you to pray about it. If you decide to ask for administration, there will be a splendid opportunity for it tonight because the prayer service will be at my home."

After some thought and prayer I indicated I would attend

the prayer service and request administration. I was greatly blessed by the prayers of the ministers. From that moment on I must admit that my leg ceased to bother me. The pain did not leave me straight away; in fact I began to wonder if the administration was going to be effective in this respect, if at all. But the point is that I wasn't worried about it anymore, though I was reluctant to make any claim of a cure. Then gradually I became aware that my leg was improving— so much so that I was to declare to my friend, "My leg is better! It doesn't trouble me anymore!" Again my faith in the church and its ordinances was strengthened and again I felt my testimony building of the glory of God and his church.

During many conversations my friend discussed with me stewardship, Zion, the revelation of God to man, baptism, etc. I was attracted to the church's belief of God revealing himself to those who trust him. I am certain that if the Saints of the church heard the actual voice of God they would not be surprised, and this is how it should be. The subject of baptism engaged my attention. While reading the book *Why I Belong* I became aware of the New Testament "rightness" of baptism by immersion which signifies one's surrender to Christ. I began to feel the very *need* of this baptism. I actually wanted it! Before I came to the knowledge of the restored church I always regarded baptism or christening by sprinkling as perfectly adequate, and thought that immersion was totally unnecessary! Twelve months prior I would have refuted any suggestion of baptism by immersion—and now I felt I needed it! Gradually, under the guidance of the young minister, I asked for baptism. On Easter Sunday of 1969 he, who under divine guidance had led me, had prayed and fasted with me, talked and written to me with patience and love unending, baptized me on that never to be forgotten morning. I actually *feel* the new person I am.

What single factor led me to the Reorganized Church of Jesus Christ of Latter Day Saints? Simply this: God gave me a friend. God spoke to me—through the life and voice of a friend. God knew whom to send. He chose carefully in his approach to me.

In all of my remarkable experience I cannot claim to have thought my way through every inch of the way, or that I even decided all things for myself. However, I am acutely aware of having been led, even when I could not clearly see the way. I trusted my heart where my mind did not fathom. I trusted God and a "gift" of spiritual discernment. All the way God has led me.

What My Husband's Conversion Did for Me

By Hazel Todd

My husband is a convert to the Reorganized Church of Jesus Christ of Latter Day Saints. In the July 1967 issue of the *Restoration Witness* he wrote of how much his new faith had changed his life—and that the change had been noted by his friends and co-workers. He told how much respect his change had brought from those with whom he worked, which surprised him for he thought that their reaction would be one of ridicule.

There are many and varied results to any religious conversion. My husband could write several testimonies which are an outgrowth of his "switch." But there is another side to see of the picture—the one from where I stand. His conversion has affected me and our life together.

One result was the happiness it brought me as one involved with a loved one in the search for truth. It was my privilege and pleasure to be a guide in his quest. I taught him the gospel as it had been taught to me from the age of ten. How thankful I was for the right answers at the right times.

Of course, our sessions were not always question and answer periods. Sometimes there were arguments as he had many preconceived ideas which took a lot of reasoning on my part. I cannot take all the credit, however. The friendliness of members, the sermons, fellowship services, plus a reunion experience he mentioned in his testimony were convincing factors.

I was so happy when my husband said, "I've got to be baptized," that tears came to my eyes. Again, when I saw him go into the waters of baptism I knew a joy too deep for words. I do not know what a man feels when he is ordained to the priesthood but I know it is a solemn and most precious moment for a wife to see the ordaining elders lay their hands on her husband's head.

Having experienced several years of being "unequally yoked to an unbeliever" as the apostle Paul so aptly stated in his second letter to the Corinthian saints I can say most fervently that it is wonderful to be married to one of like faith. To start the day with morning worship at the breakfast table and to end it with bedtime prayers, kneeling in oneness of thought, is a wonderful experience, for here is a chance to ask God's blessing and forgiveness for cross words or barbed comments which have perhaps slipped during the day.

My husband and I now both work in the church. The church encourages active participation in the Zion-building program. This was one of the things which attracted my husband to the church—the members seemed to be such an intricate part of the whole. Church as simply a Sunday affair did not appeal in the least. I feel that our faith is strengthened and our happiness intensified by such activity and duties as we are able to perform.

To me God is real and his church is true and I hope to keep our cup of joy running over.

Prayer from a Different Attitude

By Coralie M. Swick

I was one of seven children. We were not brought up in any faith, for my mother, although she was a member of the Methodist Church, believed each of us should choose for ourselves the religion we wished to embrace. We had no religious training in our home and in fact religion and righteousness seemed to be subjects to avoid in discussion.

As I grew up I embraced the Catholic faith. I believed then that one religion was as good as another according to the dictates of conscience. All were acceptable in the sight of God if you obeyed his commandments.

One of my sisters married into a family who were Reorganized Latter Day Saints. Although I could not at the time accept what she was trying to tell me, she bore her testimony well. Her life so changed that I could not help but be impressed. When she told of God's Spirit working with her tears rolled down her cheeks, and I, too, felt something. I knew that what she was saying was true. I thought it was wonderful and decided to work harder in my own faith so that I could have this experience with God.

As I look back upon my life, I can see how the Lord worked with me. I prayed diligently, but when I prayed I had little faith. I loved my heavenly Father but I wasn't sure he would answer my prayers.

The real turning point came in my life when I became pregnant with my fourth child. Doctors had warned me not to have any more children. I had had three in less than four years and all were premature. When I found I was once again pregnant I was frightened and depressed. The situation was serious, I knew. For some reason I turned to my sister and her husband for counsel. My brother-in-law was then a priest in the church. He counseled with me and told me that if I would pray with faith I would be all right.

I began to pray with a different attitude—with complete faith, believing that He would watch over me. I was willing to accept His will whatever it might be.

When it was time to go to the hospital I still had no fear, or at least I did not think I had any. I heard the nurse tell the doctor I was ready for the delivery, and at that moment I became engulfed in a fear which was so heavy upon me that I could hardly breathe. I had never known such darkness of thought. I felt a tear run down my cheek and all of a sudden I heard a voice. It was the most beautiful voice I had ever heard. It said very simply, "Coralie, everything is going to be all right." A peace came over me which I cannot now describe and which I had never felt before. The darkness was gone. I resolved then to serve my heavenly Father, to thank him always for such a wonderful blessing. I decided that as soon as I was able I would become more active in my church.

Many events took place then that led me to question and pray about my religion and what God would have me to do. I remembered a scripture my brother-in-law had read to me from James 1:5: "If any of you lack wisdom, let him ask of God, that giveth to all men liberally, and upbraideth not; and it shall be given him. But let him ask in faith, nothing wavering."

For a period of six months I prayed for direction, but I

didn't seem to get the answer I wanted. Yet events were happening that led me further away from the church to which I belonged. I wasn't going to leave the church I was in—at the risk of going to hell—unless I was positive it was what the Lord would have me do. I wanted to know truly that the Reorganized Church of Jesus Christ of Latter Day Saints was a church brought forth in the latter days by Christ himself.

I was becoming very upset over the situation when finally one night as I retired to my bed, I said to the Lord almost angrily—but mostly in desperation—"You said if I asked you, you would tell me! Why don't you tell me then?" Almost immediately I heard a voice. At first I ran from it; but, of course, I had to listen, for this was that for which I had asked. The voice said, "This church of which you pray is the true Church of Jesus Christ set on the earth." A peace came over me such as I had experienced in the hospital. I knew my answer was from God.

I united with the Reorganized Church of Jesus Christ of Latter Day Saints on Mother's Day of 1958. Since then I have had many testimonies of the divinity of this church.

I am grateful for God's love for me and for the knowledge that he leads me in the pathway of truth.

"Why Tarriest Thou?"

By Leon J. Kosmicke

My family was devout in observance of all religious rites and obligations and by virtue of my childhood

138

training (having been baptized at birth), I was unquestioning in my own devotion, willingly serving as an altar boy until I entered high school. I was complacent and satisfied to be a participant of the accepted ways of the world, and enjoyed all the habits that are commonplace among men.

I had never heard of the Reorganized Church of Jesus Christ of Latter Day Saints, but through a series of events which I now recognize as the hand of God moving to direct my life, I married into a family with a Latter Day Saint background. When the elders came to visit and talk to my wife about the "restored gospel," I would remove myself from the room. I had no objection as long as the visits excluded me.

By and by upon occasion, our son (who had been baptized into another church as a baby at my insistence) would go to church school with his mother and return home, seemingly in a happier state of mind. After some time I began to feel that I was losing him. I couldn't scold or forbid him to attend because I unwillingly liked the change which came over him as he learned about the Lord Jesus. As I had feared, one Sunday after church school he came to me and said, "Dad, may I have your permission to join Mom's church?" He was nine years old at this time and perhaps was as surprised as I at my reaction—which was one of temperance and understanding. I asked him if this was what he really wanted and upon receiving his affirmative answer I gave my permission.

As the months passed, a happy and worthwhile feeling came over me when I mentally dwelt upon the resurrection, the rebirth after the cancellation of sin, and the joy of being led by the Light of Truth. (My wife had sown seeds of the gospel at every opportunity.) I felt such a relief from not constantly dwelling on the burden of the cross, the sad thoughts of His suffering or the Crucifixion. I began to realize the full meaning of "his blood washes clean."

Yet I kept my distance from the visiting ministers. One Sunday morning, with mixed emotions of reluctance and eagerness, I attended church school with my wife and son. I liked the way the congregation treated me as a nonmember. This acceptance led to "cottage meetings" (informal presentations of the story of the church) at our home. It was easy for me to accept and believe what I heard, especially when one of the elders said to me, "If this should prove not to be the true church of Jesus Christ restored, then I take upon my soul the condemnation that would be yours." Pondering all I'd heard and learned, a strong, unkind feeling came upon me that all of this was snowballing beyond my control, that it should be slowed down, studied, and questioned. So I let go my hold on all these things that had elevated me and lifted me away from all my earlier teachings and in my heart I said, "Not yet." In spite of all the light which was given me in the meetings I looked for more proof and prayed that the Lord would prod me even more. If he did, I would be baptized.

At this point, I began to lose the enthusiasm I had felt earlier and my bright thoughts began to relax. I began to miss the joy of new anticipations and the never ending love I had felt earlier.

Finally, I found myself at an elder's home relating to him that I had never been at such a standstill in my life. I could not recapture the positive spirit that had been with me in the past. We agreed to make it a matter of earnest prayer. One day shortly thereafter as I was driving to my place of business I cried aloud to God to help me out of this stalemated condition. One block from my store a firm, positive voice spoke to me saying, through my pounding heart, "Why tarriest thou? Arise and be baptized." Those same words spoken so long ago by Ananias to Paul brought meaning and light and clear direction to my soul. I weep as the Spirit recalls to me that had I not obeyed the voice of God's counsel my doorstep might be covered with the dust of the shoes of those whom he sent.

I have no recollection of driving that one last block, parking the car, or unlocking the door. I found myself in our store dialing the pastor's home and asking for baptism in this church if he considered me worthy. It was Saturday morning and I felt it necessary that the baptism take place the following day. The pastor said, "Strangely enough, a baptismal service is planned for tomorrow evening for a woman who wishes to join with us. We will be happy to arrange for your baptism at that time." Sunday evening came and the woman was not able to participate in a beautifully and prayerfully prepared baptismal service. I was the only one baptized.

Soon I was called to the office of priest, then to the office of elder; then my son, at the age of seventeen, was called to be a priest. As an elder, after completing a series of cottage meetings at the home of a deacon whose wife was not a member, I was compelled to repeat that which was once told me: "If this should prove not to be the true church of Jesus Christ restored, then I take upon my soul the condemnation that would be yours." She was baptized and now her family, as mine, is united in the service of the Lord.

I pray that somehow this testimony may help someone who is saying "Not yet" and, through this delay, losing the prompting of the Spirit that would lead him to life everlasting in the presence of God. "Why tarriest thou?"

141

Somewhere a Group of People

By Coralie Mae Rose

Where did it all begin? I must conclude that God knew I was here all the time even while I blithely assumed that I captained my own course. My constant prayer to God was "Guide us to you," and surely but subtly we were brought through the present-day maze of religious denominations to the knowledge of which church was His.

My marriage and the birth of my first child brought a sudden realization of the tremendous debt I owed my own parents. The business of making a marriage work and rearing youngsters turned out to be far more complicated than I had expected. Personal freedom was limited to allow for a small baby and housekeeping and cooking for a busy husband, even on Sundays. What was the sense of it all? I struggled for proper perspective and, more important, I searched for divine guidance.

I sent for a pamphlet of a popular church dealing with the art of living. The answers weren't there. I turned to the direct source of the Bible. Looking back in time, I know now it was the Holy Spirit that led me to the resolution to read through the Bible. How perfect the timing when the Book of Mormon showed up on the scene shortly after I finished reading the Bible. There was no denying the truth of the Book of Mormon. Somewhere there had to be a group of people who were enjoying the same close direction the biblical Jews once had known.

The Latter Day Saints (Mormon) Church of Salt Lake City, Utah (whose missionaries presented me with the Book of Mormon), seemed a logical starting point. Certainly they had many material accomplishments. The encyclopedia showed another turn in the road that caused me to admit complete bafflement. Not only was there a Church of Jesus Christ of Latter Day Saints but there was also a *Reorganized* Church of Jesus Christ of Latter Day Saints plus many other splinter groups that appeared after the death of Joseph Smith, the martyr.

Last year we moved to Goldendale, Washington. I changed locations somewhat reluctantly, for I left behind a second term as bowling league president and an invitation to join a sorority which offered group projects, parties, and fellowship with many women my age. Yet the move seemed only fair to my husband for it shortened by a considerable distance his long drive to work.

Just about the time I had announced to the Presence who monitored my prayers that he must have picked a loser because I couldn't find the right church, a tract was delivered to our home announcing Missionary Robert O. Slasor's speaking series for the RLDS Church and another tract outlining the doctrines of the church. How right they seemed.

My husband had been called to the bedside of his desperately ill father, thus leaving me free to attend the first few sermons of the series. Some time later, I discovered our area had been tracted only at the last minute when the priesthood members handling the task learned their supper would be delayed.

From this first contact with the church and with my husband's consent and support, I was baptized four months later. This first chapter may have taken ten years to accomplish, but it has been a precious gift from God. And it is only the beginning.

A Testimony of the Book of Mormon

By Cecil R. Ettinger

In 1953 I held a missionary series which included a cottage meeting each week in the home of a very intelligent young man who was deeply concerned about the gospel. As I went through the standard presentations, we talked about the purpose of Christ's church, its history of apostasy and reformation, and the coming forth of the Restoration movement.

On one particular evening, I talked about the Book of Mormon. As had been my custom to this time in cottage meeting work, the first presentation centered on the use of archaeological evidence to prove that Joseph Smith could not have written such a book from his own abilities. I talked about the nature of the people who populated the land of the Americas prior to the coming of Christ in Palestine and discussed the cultural level, ethnic possibilities, religious potential, and evident history of these people.

After a very stimulating conversation, the young man finally turned to me and said, "Do you know anything about the archaeology of the Bible?" By coincidence I had just taken a course on biblical archaeology from the North Central Seminary at Naperville, Illinois, which is sponsored by the Evangelical United Brethren Church. Immediately I responded to his question by discussing some of my studies and referring to manuscripts, diggings, and current theories being expounded. Finally, he asked me another question: "What convinced you of the divinity of the Bible? Did archaeology prove to you that the Bible was true?" I bore my testimony by stating that I had believed in the scriptures as contained in the Holy Bible long before I knew anything about biblical archaeology. I was convinced of the divinity of the scriptures because of the teachings contained therein and by the accompanying testimony of the Holy Spirit as I read it. I talked briefly about the life of Jesus, the Sermon on the Mount, the teachings of the apostle Paul, and some of the more obvious passages of the Bible.

He then turned to me and said, "Now tell me about the Book of Mormon."

I immediately saw his point and began to bear witness of what had convinced me of the truth of the Book of Mormon. I spoke of the character of Nephi, the son of Lehi, and how under most adverse circumstances of physical privation and fraternal jealousy he still served the Lord in truth. I bore witness of the worship experience of Enos as he went to pray and found the Lord in his life. I naturally referred to the great King Benjamin and to his sermon. One of my favorite passages had always been the testimony of Amulek as he silenced the queries of Zeezrom with the marvelous testimony of the nature of baptism contained in the eighth chapter. I concluded my own testimony with Moroni's:

"Yea, come unto Christ, and be perfected in him, and deny yourselves of all ungodliness; if ye shall deny yourselves of all ungodliness, and love God with all your might, mind and strength, then is his grace sufficient for you, that by his grace ye may be perfect in Christ; and if by the grace of God ye are perfect in Christ, ye can in no wise deny the power of God."

My friend then turned to me and requested to be baptized in Christ's name.

From that time until now I have appreciated the place of archaeology in the study of the Book of Mormon, but I have had a continual and growing conviction of the words of truth that are between its covers. The experiences and testimonies of those who have communicated to us through the written word are accompanied by the convicting witness of the Holy Spirit.

Permission to View

By Gerald L. Sooter

It is not often that a person with good health, financial security, happy family life, and a prosperous future desires to leave this mortal life. On the other hand, it is not often that one glimpses the beauty of eternity from 30,000 feet above the earth.

There seems to be a time in life when man feels a need for something greater than that possible for him to attain. Not always do these occasions reflect a physical need, for my depressed soul at this time needed a spiritual lift.

Depression is something that can destroy man. I had been asking myself, "What is it that causes men to hate and despise each other? Why do we search for the faults of others to justify our own? What is missing in our lives? What can I do?" It was in such spirit that I boarded an airplane on a rainy morning.

The plane, filled mostly with businessmen, had to taxi across three runways to its holding area. Suddenly, in the middle of a runway, the pilot slammed on the brakes as another plane flew directly in front of us. We had escaped a dangerous collision in which we all could have been killed. Fortunately, no one was injured.

As the plane rose through a thick rain-cloud formation, the craft seemed all alone as I peered through small round windows and saw only its wing tips. For thirty minutes all that was visible were gloomy rain clouds. A half hour of gloominess was all I needed to again drive me into a state of depression. I turned to the Lord in silent prayer, asking that I be permitted to receive an understanding of the problems that caused my depression.

Suddenly the sunlight broke through the rain clouds and seemingly focused on me through the tiny window where I sat. It was the most beautiful thing I've ever experienced. A feeling of warmth seemed to begin at my head, working downward, until it reached my toes. Without thinking, I turned toward a fellow passenger to exclaim, "Isn't it beautiful," but refrained when I sensed he would not understand.

The unusual warmth increased as the craft finally flew out of the cloud formation, enabling me to see creation at 30,000 feet. I silently uttered my thanks to God for being permitted to view something "extra" in the beauty of his dwelling place. I prayed: "Father, what is the answer to my depressed soul? How can I establish rapport with my fellowman? How can I work in thy kingdom?" I was overcome as the unusual warmth continued to envelop me and I humbly uttered, "Lord, let me come and live with you now.. . ." Immediately, the warmth seemed to burn within my soul as words were strongly impressed upon my mind: "Have patience, my son. Love your brother even as I have loved you."

One man alone cannot build castles. So it is in building Christianity within one's own life. My questions were answered. My life had been changed because of God's love for me. By the same token, a sincere love for my fellowman could result only in something happening in their lives as well as my own. Exhibiting patience is not always easy, but it always exists when godly love is present.

Man does not have to go to 30,000 feet to find God or to glimpse the beauty of his dwelling place. God will find man anywhere when man humbly responds to God's basic nature of love.

God's Forceful Presence

By Edna Daniels

When someone speaks of a testimony I always feel that this is an undeniable communication with our Maker that no amount of rationalization can discount. As I reevaluate experiences, I must know beyond doubt that they are a direct communication between God and me—a direct intervention on his part, not some natural result which in my own zeal I overemphasize. I hope this tendency to be overly cautious does not reflect unfavorably on my testimony of his ever present love and concern in my life as evidenced by the two which follow.

I applied and was accepted as a nursing student in a hospital in Saskatoon, Saskatchewan. Shortly before, Brother Z. Z. Renfroe, an appointee minister of the church, baptized me. I wanted to attend the "San," the church school of nursing, but in my financial condition even the idea was ridiculous. However, I prayed about it and felt that my desire and plan were pleasing to God.

At this time I was living with Brother and Sister Ireland. Gladys Ireland was not only my best friend but had introduced me to the church. When my parents rejected me she and her family opened their home to me, feeding and sheltering me and loving me in a way that even now brings tears of love and gratitude to my eyes. They were my "family" and they hold the special place in my heart that each of us reserves for our father and mother, sisters and brothers. So often when I wonder how I can witness effectively I am reminded of their unselfish love and realize again that simply loving those to whom we are trying to witness is a greater witness than anything we can say. They and all the other Saints in the congregation were praying that it would be possible for me to go to the "San." Despite this, however, everything went wrong, and I began to wonder if it was what the Lord wanted me to do after all.

One afternoon at a women's department meeting, I was sitting with a hymnbook in my lap and chanced to look down. The words "Go to Zion" were the only words I noticed. I chided myself for being so dramatic about my problems and closed the book, directing my attention elsewhere. A few minutes later I felt compelled to look down again at what I supposed to be a closed book. To my surprise the book was again open, and again the words "Go to Zion" were all that I could see. I closed the book, a little less determinedly than before. This compulsion to look down again occurred once more, and this time I saw the words "Go to Zion—happily." I was rather perturbed by this time, but decided that it was utter nonsense. The hymnal had somehow just fallen open, and after all, I reasoned, no matter where you looked in the hymnal the words "Go to Zion" were bound to appear. I leafed through it again and again, opening it and closing it, until I was tired and frustrated. Nowhere was I able to find the mention of Zion, let alone the actual words which I had seen. Disturbed, but still doubting, I again closed the hymnal and laid it down while meditating on what had just transpired. While lost in my thoughts, I happened to glance down and was quite shaken as I read the words of a hymn, "Where wilt thou put thy trust, in a frail form of clay?"

The road to the "San" was no less difficult than it had been before—in fact, it became even harder. There were times when even some of the Saints said, "It doesn't look like you are going to make it, Edna." As doubting as my nature was, however, I never once doubted that I would go. I knew I would and despite what seemed to be insurmountable barriers, I did.

My timing wasn't all it could have been, but I didn't want to wait one day more after I was cleared to go. I'd had such a hard time getting that far I didn't want any further problems. So I went from a very cold Canadian spring into one of the hottest summers Kansas City, Missouri, had had in thirty years. In the first week of June 1954 I stepped off the train into a 100 degree plus temperature dressed in a heavy wool suit.

Since my finances were meager (and even more so after the expense of getting my visa) I planned to work until September when school started. I obtained work readily, but the unaccustomed heat made me so weak and sick (I lost twenty pounds in a week) that I had to quit. Meanwhile the rent didn't stop and so by September I had almost no money left.

I had a Rotary loan for my tuition and since my meals and room were provided by the school, I felt I could manage on what I had—coupled with any baby-sitting jobs I could get. I hadn't considered the many little items that we never think of unless we are literally counting pennies, such as soap, facial tissue, etc. Before long I realized I was fighting a losing battle and I turned to the only one I knew—God. I begged him to help me. After all, I reasoned, I knew he wanted me to come here, so I was confident of his care. The days passed and the baby-sitting was scarce. There were many girls available for baby-sitting. Finally, the day came when I was literally down to my last penny and I went to the nursing office to make arrangements to drop out for a while to work. I decided I couldn't do much with a penny anyway and so I put my last penny in the penny gum machine.

At the office I was told that there was some financial aid for student nurses. Elated, I inquired as to how and when this money had to be repaid. It didn't have to be repaid. The only condition to be met was that the receiver was to help someone else. This was lovely sentiment and I suppose financial assistance on this basis once or twice might be acceptable, but I was facing a period of three years during which I would need help. I was thankful to the anonymous donor—it's nice to know that someone is this kind and thoughtful—but I just couldn't accept all the help I needed on that basis. I was told to think about it. I headed back to the dormitory wondering what to do.

On the way I stopped for my mail. There was a letter in my box—a letter which contained a money order for one hundred dollars. I was so grateful for God's never ceasing love for me and for the Saints who were so attuned to him that they were always "about their Father's business"! As I read the letter I was aware of God's gentle but forceful presence in the lives of those who loved and followed him.

The letter was from a man and his wife who said they had felt they should help me in some way. They had discussed helping me and then had forgotten about it. One day, he said, while he was in his office, he felt there was something to do but he didn't know what. The feeling was so great that he knelt in prayer and was told to send me some money and offer me financial assistance. I was happy but not surprised, because I knew God would take care of me. How I didn't know. If I had quit for a year or so, it would not have been because he had abandoned me; it would have been but part of his plan. I was grateful that this wasn't to be, however; but I was more grateful for this family who placed God above all else and had the faith it required to take the savings for their children's education and send it to me monthly. They would not allow me to pay interest and the loan was payable when and how I could afford to repay it. Although I have seen this family but rarely over the years, my heart is full of gratitude to them and all the others who opened their homes, families, and very hearts to a girl of no special talent and even less worth, simply because of their love for the Master.

Grand Canyon Caravan

By John R. Ferguson

During the summer of 1967 youth of the San Bernardino District of California continued in their planned endeavor of fellowship and corporate witness for the second time. All of this was made possible through the enthusiasm of several young people during a spring camping retreat of 1966. In the course of the activity several felt the desire to accomplish more than the normal labors of life and to overcome the humdrum of casual activity. They committed themselves to one of the most ambitious endeavors I have ever witnessed: A desire to share the goodness of Christ that had come into their lives with those beyond their small circle.

The result of this encounter with the Master developed into an evangelistic cause which was to become known as the

"Grand Canyon Caravan." It was an opportunity for the teen-agers to show that they could serve Christ with tremendous vitality and quality of life.

The theme for the caravan of 1967 was "Standards of Sainthood." The young people were finding out that the Christian life required work and discipline rather than complacency. It would never do to sit idly by and criticize society for its inequities, shortcomings, and standards. If our world was to become a better place to live, it would transpire only through the efforts of concerned Christians and not a group of complaining young rebels. For this reason many of the Leaguers invited and encouraged their friends to share with them the task of building the kingdom.

We departed from the Riverside Church aboard buses, and the first stop was at Barstow, California, where the women's department met seventy-seven hungry youth with a delicious luncheon. And while we are giving credit to the adults, the crowning sacrifice was made by Anna May Hoach and Erma Patella who consented to be the camp cooks for the entire trip. This required cooking over Coleman stoves for seventy-seven ambitious eaters, many of whom ate twice the normal diet of adults.

If I live to be one hundred years old, I shall never forget the expression on the faces of these two fine women when we stepped off the air-conditioned buses near the edge of the Colorado River on the Mojave Desert. There was sand as far as the eyes could see in any direction, not a tree in sight, and the temperature was a "moderate" 122 degrees Fahrenheit. Their sacrifice did not go unnoticed, however, for seventy-seven young people attested to this by the often stated phrase, "Is there any more?"

All of the young people pitched in to make the camping adventure a success, but eight young men in particular added some extra spark. Help was needed in counseling and worship activities. These eight, ranging in age from seventeen through twenty and all ministers, gave of their time unselfishly to the success of the camp worship services. Great assistance was rendered by these young ministers to the eight counselors and camp nurse. To observe these young men stand before their peers in witness of Christ made your heart "skip a beat."

Wednesday was our last full day of camping at the Colorado River and that afternoon amidst the grandeur of the desert we had a baptismal service. For several present it culminated one year's labor in witnessing, and the Spirit was present in abundance. My heart was filled with joy as I stood in the water overlooking the crowd of young people gathered at the edge of the river. Not one was told that attendance was required but by self-choice all seventy-seven were present.

We sang a hymn, "Afar in Old Judea." We added a closing verse for the specific occasion in which we were sharing that day. The words rolled across the water:

"Afar in old Judea, above the Jordan stream
A heavenly light descended on a baptismal scene.
Then came the confirmation of Jesus from above.
The sacramental signet: The Spirit as a dove. . . .
Here in God's holy presence we come this day to share
With those who made their promise with outstretched arms
    in prayer.
Near to the edge of nature this great expanse we see,
As once again we covenant our hearts and lives to Thee."

The love of the Master abounded, for as I stood in the water to receive the candidates, I again looked over the group gathered on the bank of the river and not one eye was dry. In the congregation were several football and wrestling letter-men, some who felt that social clubs were the "in thing," some who in previous months had been in trouble with the law, and many others of varied backgrounds. But today they were all one in the "community of believers." After the service one young woman, sensing the magnitude of the gospel, asked for baptism and that night we were to share once again in a baptismal service.

The campfire had been planned around a theme offering opportunity for dedication. Every camper was given the chance to make his commitment for service in the kingdom task. In the stillness of the night each one lighted a candle and placed it on a cross. The burning cross was launched out into the river and as it slowly floated away we all joined together in the baptismal service. The same Spirit was once again abundantly present as in the earlier service. The next morning we boarded our buses and left for the rim of the canyon.

The week seemed a few fleeting hours when Friday night arrived. Many experiences and feelings had yet to be shared and the early morning service planned for Saturday would not give us sufficient time. Two services were scheduled, therefore, one at sunset Friday for the confirmation of those baptized earlier in the week and a dedication service at sunrise Saturday morning.

The youth came worthily prepared to these services, for they well knew the meaning and significance of participating in a community of believers. The confirmation service was held on a rock at the canyon's edge seven thousand feet above the valley floor. Grandeur Point is the name given this place and the word barely describes the magnificent view. An expanse of fifteen miles separated us from the other side of the canyon and from our vantage point we could look to the left, right, or straight ahead without obstruction. Just as the sun was setting in the west and the vivid colors of purple, red, orange, and blue danced on the canyon's walls, the young souls were confirmed into the Church of Jesus Christ. Many prayers ascended that night, for love abounded in the fellowship of young Saints about their Father's work.

The youth were now ready to reach out and grasp more of the eternal nature. An opportunity was extended the young people to assist the Zion's League of Tahiti in purchasing surfboards for their youth activities. The Tahitian League had worked for many months to purchase surfboards but the cost of shipping had been considerably more than anticipated, so the caravaners took upon themselves the joy of world outreach. There would be no money-raising projects—just the sacrifice of personal funds which many had planned to spend on souvenirs and refreshments. The offering was taken the last day of the camp. Their experiences had not been superficial, for more than the required amount was received and the love of the Master crossed the ocean through the hearts of young people.

Five-thirty o'clock was the waking hour Saturday morning, for it was a half-hour walk to the canyon and our sunrise dedication service. This day the heavenly Father was pleased and all heaven rejoiced, for every heart and mind was touched with his Spirit. A one-hour service had been planned in hopes of returning to the campsite for breakfast by seven thirty. We had a long journey home. Nearly everyone wanted to share in the service, however, and the two-hour mark was passed unnoticed. Words are inadequate to describe the warmth, the fellowship, the concern, and the desire to be steadfast of purpose among the youth that morning.

We sang a hymn to conclude the service and camping activity, one which would grasp the magnitude and abundance of the power present within our midst. A verse was added to the hymn, "O Master, Let Me Walk with Thee," to instill added meaning to the worship experience.

"Here at the canyon's edge we pray, to consecrate our lives
    this day.

May this great vision we behold strengthen and guide us in
Thy fold."

We then shared in a closing prayer of consecration. For
the first time in my life I witnessed teen-agers desiring to
remain in worship and meditation rather than scamper to the
frolics of life. The two hours which were evolving into three
were spent sitting on solid rock without chairs or cushions.
Yet all remained reluctant to leave this fellowship. Throughout the week many had wrestled with the problems of life.
Some had come to new insights by their own choice; some
chose to chart a new course in life. I am confident when I
say, this week the Lord spoke through the lives of these
young witnesses. Because of this experience they shall never
be the same.

As I reflect on the several dynamic experiences of my
life, two profound truths are always manifest. Each
apprehension has been occasioned by a vigorous encounter
with the Divine and without exception every experience
always involved other people. There have been times when
the climactic event was spent alone but always this
apprehension was made possible through the sacrifice of
others.

Our greatest opportunities for witness are always in the
corporate endeavor. We stand strong in the strength of others
through the community of believers. One of the counselors
to the president of the church, M. L. Draper, very aptly
shares in one of his books the thesis of this story and
experience of these youth.

"When people of good intent are together they do
better than when alone. Righteous people strengthen
each other in fellowship. They multiply each other's
strength. There are also some sinful situations of group
nature which can only be changed by group action. That
is why repentant individuals need to be associated

157

together in the fellowship of the kingdom of God on earth. This is the social manifestation of repentance. It is a process of spiritual evolution in individuals and in groups, eliminating evil and the second best in favor of the better and the best in life purposes and habits.

"This is a program of personal and social spiritual growth which develops personal strength and ability and skills and moral power and social righteousness. Such a way of life has both the design of beauty and utility and the quality which will endure forever."

There are many oceans yet uncharted in spiritual dynamics, waiting for dedicated Christians to launch their lives for Christ in the sea of humanity. In a world where countless thousands are spiritually drowning each day, a call for service is sounded. These young people stood in witness and met the challenge of the ages.

In a period of just fourteen months, sixteen people entered the waters of baptism through the efforts of these young men and women. Ten were baptized on the caravans and six in their home congregations. Truly the harvest was beyond expectation, for more was garnered than bringing friends into the community of believers. Now many young people have a testimony that some adults never grasp throughout their lives.

The Road to True Nobility

By Mercedes Vaughn

I was born of nobility in Paris, France, among luxury and plenty. I was the only child of the family. When I was five months old, I lost my parents in a car accident, and I was raised by my grandmother. I was educated in the finest private schools of France, Switzerland, and Spain.

Strangely enough, even at the age of eight years, I knew I did not believe in the teachings of the church in which I had been baptized. Nevertheless, I believed in God and prayed constantly to find the "right way." I swore in my heart that I would never marry anyone of my religion, even though this was the desire of my family.

Since I was not free to pick my friends (everywhere I went I was accompanied by a governess) I joined the Girl Scouts and became very active. I found from this association that not everyone had life so easy.

At a Girl Scouts Jamboree held in Paris in 1945, following World War II, I met a girl by the name of Sally, from Massachusetts, U.S.A. After the Jamboree, we corresponded and became good pen pals for several years, until Sally married and could not keep up correspondence. Since I still wanted to correspond with someone in the United States, Sally gave my name to a woman editor whom she knew. The editor printed my picture and a short description in *Girl Friend* magazine. Anyone who wished to correspond could write me in care of the editor. The editor forwarded the letters, leaving it up to me if I wanted to answer.

So it was that on a rainy Sunday afternoon in the lobby of a hotel in Meridian, Mississippi, a young man who was in town on business was standing by the magazine rack. He picked up this particular issue of *Girl Friend* magazine (the magazine had a rather limited circulation) and found my name. He had been searching for a person who knew French, with whom he could correspond to help learn the language. His enthusiasm for learning French was short-lived when I became adept at English. Futhermore, he hated to write letters. In one of his letters, however, George Vaughn invited me to come to the United States.

It took three long years to clear the red tape (both my family's and the government's) for my visit. In the meantime his invitaion to visit turned into a proposal of marriage. After three years people get to know each other pretty well. And so it was that love, almost before either of us realized it, had found its place in our lives.

We were engaged by correspondence—the ring arrived in a letter. When I announced I was going to the United States, my family frowned; but when I announced I was getting married to a Protestant, "the walls fell in," and from that day on I was disowned by my family. I signed papers giving up any claim to the family title or fortune. When I boarded the plane for the United States, I was a penniless girl going to a strange land with a new language, new ways of life—new everything.

Life held new adventures. I did not speak English, George did not speak French, so we resorted to pen and paper.

The customs, the ways of life, were very different even in the method of eating. I had always eaten on silver plates, and the shock was great when I saw that in the United States people ate even on paper plates! The first few years were a great trial for me.

There were additions to our family and as people do when children begin to mature, our thoughts turned toward God and rearing children in a church.

George was employed as a research physicist at Midwest Research Institute in Kansas City. There he came in contact with Bill Clow, a fellow worker and a priesthood member in the Reorganized Church of Jesus Christ of Latter Day Saints. One noon hour he learned about the Book of Mormon in a discussion with Bill and mentioned that he would like to read the book. However, his intention for reading was to make conversation and ridicule it. Next day, Bill brought a copy of the book and that night George sat down to glance through it. As he was reading the second page a voice spoke to him and said: "This is no book to take lightly or to ridicule." From that moment on the Book of Mormon held an inspired and divine interest. Soon Bill Clow and Elder Everett Jones of Sterling Avenue congregation in Independence held cottage meetings in our home.

One night I told George that I did not want to discuss religion because I had been forced into religion all my life. I did not believe and now I resisted all churches. Nevertheless George prayed that I would see things as he had discovered them in reading the Book of Mormon. We were expecting our second child, and on Thanksgiving Day of 1957 I was ill. I was resting on the bed silently praying to God. In answer to my prayer, the Lord Jesus appeared, and with his appearance the sickness went away.

Now that I had seen Him and knew that he lived, I had confirmation that this was his church. In January 1958 my husband and I were baptized. Because of my knowledge of French and Spanish, Apostle Charles Hield asked me to translate tracts into these languages. I assisted in the translation of the Book of Mormon into Spanish and later translated it into French. At the present I am assisting with the translation of the Doctrine and Covenants into Spanish.

Our family enjoys church life very much; the people are wonderful and they have been an inspiration to me. I am very thankful for the opportunity and privilege of serving in a small way.

To Seek the Spirit

By Dorothy Magnuson

My parents as well as my grandparents were very spiritual people. We were of modest means but there were always good books to read including encyclopedias and the scriptures.

I married the son of a minister of a denomination different than my own. When we were first dating, his father told him not to set foot in my church because if he did the devil "would get hold of him." But our dating became serious and, in time, we were married.

During the first few years of marriage, my husband had to work Sundays and we could not attend church together. In nine months our first son was born and a second son twenty-one months later. We were just barely getting by financially and there were problems of every nature. There were happy moments, although as a whole it was not a particularly happy time.

When the second world war began my husband went to work in a shipyard. In a few years galvanized poison had destroyed his lungs. During the last year of his life, he developed tuberculosis but for some reason the doctor did not discover the condition. He was in and out of the hospital until finally he was dismissed even though he had trouble breathing. About two weeks before my husband's death he had so much trouble breathing that in desperation he went to another doctor. After the test the doctor ordered my husband to enter a sanitarium. The two boys and I were checked and found to have shadows. I was placed in a hospital until the baby came. My husband died when I was eight months pregnant with our third son. As soon as the baby was born, I was transferred to a sanitarium. I was allowed to see my third son from the door of my hospital room as a sister-in-law took him home with her. The two older boys had gone to my parents' home to stay.

I was confined to my bed for the first few months. I don't think I have to tell you how I suffered mentally as well as physically. The saying that work is a boon or a blessing for one who is mourning a lost loved one is surely true, and the saying that time heals all wounds is true only if you have the healing therapy of work, which in my case was denied. Above all I did not have the "balm of Gilead" spoken of in the hymn "Did You Think to Pray," so I was given a harmless looking little white pill. Eight months later when I was released to my parents' home I discovered that I had become addicted to the medicine in the pill.

I was not allowed much activity for some time, but even the little I could do helped some during the day. I will never forget the nights I spent in such agony that it was physical as well as mental. When in desperation I asked the doctors for help, they said all they could do was give me more of the same pills. I refused them.

My parents were faithful members of the church. During this terrible time of trial and turmoil I picked up the Book of Mormon which was lying on a table in the living room, and began to read. Why I picked it up I will never know because I was not interested in it. As I opened it and read, a warm, peaceful feeling came over me. It is very hard to describe correctly and in detail, but I doubt if I will ever forget it.

Shortly after this incident my parents asked me if I would like to go to reunion with them. It was held on the shore of a beautiful lake nearby. I was all for it since I loved to swim and I looked forward to it as a recreational vacation.

One evening in the course of that week, however, I sat

listening to a very gifted speaker. I was not listening intently, but even so I became fascinated with the polished way he used words. Then that same warm, peaceful feeling entered my being as it had before. Under its influence I commenced thinking of ways I might live a better life and above all how I might be a better mother. I remember how eager I was for knowledge and how I began to pray for direction for myself as well as for my boys. I know now that this was the Spirit of Christ that John spoke of in the fourteenth chapter of his writing. Another such scripture is found in the tenth chapter of Romans.

"How shall they believe in him of whom they have not heard? and how shall they hear without a preacher? . . . As it is written, How beautiful are the feet of them that preach the gospel of peace, and bring glad tidings of good things! So then faith cometh by hearing, and hearing by the word of God."

In the quiet peace of this good feeling I found the Christ.

It Is Not Ye That Speak

By Frank M. Solina

For many years I went to church because I was told to go by my parents. Later various activities, such as an orchestra, enticed me to attend. I played in the orchestra and often became involved in other functions just to see how far I could go without actually joining. Then thirty years ago my mother died and I went to live with a friend of my mother's. She asked me to go to her church which I did, but with the same malice and intent as before. I expected the same situation as at other times, but here I found something that I hadn't expected.

The people accepted me as one of them from the first meeting. Even their attitude was different. As time passed I became interested in playing in the band and I sang in the choir. I attended the youth group which they called Zion's League, and I met a girl. She was and still is the most lovely person I have ever met. Later she became my wife.

About the time the war in Vietnam started something happened and I became mean and argumentive. I would deliberately ridicule my wife and "her" church. Often I would swear at her and condemn the church and its "quacking." It reached a culminating point when I told her to make a choice of me or her friends in the church. Before she had to make this decision one of those things happened that makes a tremendous difference in a person's life. I was transferred from one coast to the other.

Following my transfer the Lord came into my life. In one of his sure but mysterious ways he overcame my bitterness. On the first Sunday in our new home my wife said she was going to church. For some unknown reason I said I would go with her. We drove to the church some twenty miles away; and although we contended with one-way streets in an unfamiliar area, we arrived on time. As Brother Heap, the pastor, and I clasped hands we experienced that electrifying presence of the Holy Spirit. We were shrouded in light and our very beings were warmed. Our minds became one.

This man and I spent many hours talking together under the influence of this spirit. There was such a oneness between us that we could actually "feel" each other's thoughts and desires.

I was baptized at a reunion in Onset, Massachusetts, in July of 1964. Under the influence of this experience my life as a tyrant was replaced with a deep concern for humanity. My motivations and attitudes were caught up in compassion for my fellowman. Other officers in my military unit made light of my change and joked about me "going soft in my old age." But the change could be measured, for my new attitude was part of the reason for my department being awarded the Navy "E" of excellence for two different years. My changed attitude toward the men under my command received their consideration.

Then one night Brother Heap telephoned to see if I was going to be home and if he could stop by. I knew that he was coming to ask me to accept a call to the priesthood. I told him that it was all right to come, and as I hung up the phone I told my wife why I thought he was coming. I accepted the call and dedicated my life to Christ. A short time after the call we moved to Wilmington, California, and there received orders for Vietnam.

When I arrived at DaNang in Vietnam, Brother Del Cory, the RLDS chaplain, was making ready to leave. We met at the airfield and he asked me if I would take over his responsibilities. I had been a member of the church and priesthood for such a short time that I accepted with a deep feeling of inadequacy.

As the "minister" for RLDS servicemen in Vietnam, I have had many experiences. One time I went into a camp seeking one of our members and found him talking with some of his buddies. We chatted for a while and then I told him who I was and what my job was. The other men became deeply interested and joined in the conversation. At the end of our talk one of the men asked if we could pray. We prayed and the glorious presence of the Master was with us. As I turned to board the helicopter, one of the men came to me and said, "Lieutenant, I have never felt there was a God. Thanks for coming." I wept, for all of a sudden the full impact of Matthew 10:20 came to me and I realized the significance of the Holy Spirit. "For it is not ye that speak, but the spirit of your Father which speaketh in you." My life was one of newfound joy and love.

On Christmas Day after the services were held, I was stricken with a heart attack. Just before this happened I was patting myself on the back for really holding a good service—then it happened. I had completely and undeniably forgotten Christ and put myself first. In such a short time I had forgotten the instructions of Matthew. I suffered endless torture for five days. When I once again became rational, I prayed for God's forgiveness and for his strength. I felt I could not ask God to help me through my torment because I had denied him. But God, being the merciful God that he is, spared my life and made me know that no man is above his Master.

On June 30, 1967, I was retired from the service with a medical disability. I intend and desire to serve my God and do all in my power to let people know of his mercy and forgiveness and the beautiful and abundant life available through accepting his gospel. I am free to pursue my work for the Master.

Face to Face

By Carole Ann Mead

As I sit to write this experience, I find myself filling my lungs with air, lifting my eyes toward heaven, and remembering when breathing was nearly impossible for me.

My husband and I were stationed in Florida in 1960 with

our two children. Being from Florida originally, we found this very exciting, for we had always enjoyed water sports and were looking forward to enjoying them here for two years.

We became quite involved in organizing a scuba (self-contained underwater breathing apparatus) diving club on our base. Not having used an aqualung, I was put on the beginner's list for instruction. When I had advanced to where my husband was confident that I was a safe diver, he bought me an aqualung. We placed particular emphasis on safety training and had some very well-trained divers who did the instructing. I had an extensive "checkout," with one of the other divers as instructor, and went to my first competitive spearfishing meet.

The club traveled to a nearby town for a weekend of diving and fellowship with divers from many parts of the South. Spirits were high and each one felt that he would win the big trophy that year! I was as anxious as the rest to get started.

Competition was held nine miles out in the Gulf of Mexico at the site of a sunken Russian freighter. A Navy tugboat provided transportation for the ninety-minute trip to the freighter.

The first day of diving was enjoyable, but few fish were shot. The second day was another story. There were fish everywhere! Divers were boating their fish before I was ready to enter the water. I made several dives with my "buddy" (an absolute necessity for all divers) and we rested between dives. The day was coming to a close and I still had not boated a fish. I decided to make one more dive.

As I submerged I saw that my buddy was just below me, my husband was beside me, and his buddy was directly under him. When I reached a depth of sixty feet I saw a school of fish swimming toward us, and I quickly moved in their direction and shot one. I was thrilled at having shot the fish and swam back to my husband. My intention was to show the fish to him and my buddy, surface, and register my catch with the judges. As I approached my fellow divers there was a "new" diver among them. He was acting strangely and was giving the diver's hand signal that he was out of air and needed help. My husband quickly came to his aid by giving him his mouthpiece to "buddy-breathe" (each diver alternating a breath from the same regulator). The new diver looked very strange. His eyes were panic-stricken and I was afraid. I saw that he did not intend to return my husband's mouthpiece. I tapped my husband and signaled that I would buddy-breathe with him to the surface. When the stranger saw my mouthpiece being offered, he dropped my husband's and took mine. Instead of buddy-breathing, however, he started for the surface, dragging me with him. We were rocketing up! I remember the bubbles, the spear gun cable tangled around me, flying upward, the panicked eyes through the bubbles, my rapid breathing, and—no air! When my husband realized what was taking place, he tried to surface ahead of us to assure that we did not surface under the tug. At the rate of speed we were traveling, we most surely would have been injured.

As we ascended through the dark water and I looked upward into the sun rays, I knew that the surface was near . . . ten or twelve feet more. "Oh, dear God," I prayed, "please don't let us all die!" Then through the bubbles a different face—my buddy! Through this maze came a friendly smile and a regulator. Air! I blew hard into the mouthpiece to clear out the water so that I could breathe. Good sweet air.

We popped out of the water in a tangled mess of cable and fish. My husband and buddy were with me and the strange diver was still gasping through my regulator, even though we were on the surface.

The first realization that I might be injured came when I realized that I could not fill my lungs. I thought that this was due to the excitement and waited a short time before saying anything to my companions. However, it was soon apparent that I needed help. I told them that I was having difficulty in breathing. My buddy wrestled my regulator from the strange diver and put it into my mouth. It was easier to breathe, but I still could not fill my lungs. My husband called for a dinghy from the tug and the sailors quickly got one to us. As they approached I laboriously followed their orders: "Unbuckle your weights." "Drop your tanks." "Give me your gun." I can only imagine being pulled into the dinghy, and I only vaguely remember being hauled aboard the tug.

Gray! Everything was gray! I was lying somewhere and could see shadows above me. The shadows seemed to be people. They were saying things to which I was unable to respond. "If we can just get her back down she'll be all right." "If you can hear me, just move your head." But I could not move my head. I could hear well, but could see only gray shadows.

I remained in this state for what seemed to be ages. My first clear sight came at the sudden jolt of being lifted off the deck in a stretcher which dangled at the end of a long cable attached to a helicopter. I was raised into the 'copter and as we made for shore was able to give a few details to a doctor who was on board. The pain was unbearable in my left arm and chest. I was still paralyzed, but had some reasoning power and could recount the occurrences in a somewhat intelligible manner. Unconsciousness seemed to be a blessing and was my only relief from that terrible pain. I wanted to ask, "Am I going to die?" but was too afraid of the answer. I had come face-to-face with my Master under that water, and now I could only hope that He had seen my need. I may have prayed again, but I can't remember. All I know is that I was very close to him. When you're that close, perhaps you don't need to pray.

On shore the doctor and I were placed in a pressurized aircraft and flown at low level to the Naval recompression chamber at Panama City, Florida. A Naval hospital corpsman, a specialist in diving diseases, was my companion in this five-foot cylinder, eight feet long, with two portholes. Before my thirty-eight hours were up in the chamber I began to recognize people by their noses.

The big question: diagnosis! "What's wrong with her?" "She can't have the bends, for she wasn't down long enough." "And air embolism is out. At sixty feet she would be dead!"

In air embolism the lung ruptures and air gets into the bloodstream. The lung rupture is caused by a rapid ascent without exhaling. The air that escapes through the rupture moves through the bloodstream and usually into the brain, killing the victim instantly. I recalled that I did not exhale on ascent, so my lungs should have exploded like balloons. The only exhale that I made was just before the surface when I cleared my buddy's regulator for air. The Navy divers and doctors said that I would have been dead before then if I had had an embolism. The Naval experimental diving school at Key West, Florida, was contacted by telephone as was the Naval diving school in Washington, D.C. Neither school could give any reasons for my being alive.

The divers and doctors decided that they would simulate the depth at which I was injured. If I responded by having the pain ease, they would follow a table indicating the depth which must be simulated in the chamber for my recovery. They treated me for air embolism, knowing that it could not be so.

The recompression chamber uses air instead of water to pressurize its occupants. The depth in the chamber was set at 60 feet. I responded and was then taken to a pressurized depth of 165 feet. The pressure was decreased in stages, thus working the "foreign" air out of my body. After completely depressurizing, I was taken to Tyndall AFB Hospital where I was given an EKG and lung X ray. I was treated for coronary occlusion and kept in bed for five weeks.

During these weeks a missionary from my husband's home branch, one hundred miles away, came to visit with me often. I was not a member of the Reorganized Church of Jesus Christ of Latter Day Saints at that time. We spent much time talking, and he assured me that what had happened to me was not a disaster and that I would recover. I shall ever be grateful for these visits and the prayers that we shared together.

After hospitalization I was allowed to go home on very limited activity and could visit my children, who were being cared for by their grandparents in another town, only on weekends.

I had to start thinking when people *seriously* said that I had a guardian angel. Angel? Yes, perhaps this was possible. After all, the doctors could find every reason for my death but not one for my life. A miracle? Yes, I suppose it was.

When I decided that what had happened could not be coincidence, I came face-to-face with my Master again. He had given me a guardian angel. He had saved me from an early death. What was I going to do about it? Some gratitude to God if I remained my old self! I could not continue the life I had known until this time. I made a decision to change and began by reading the scriptures of my husband's church—and to associate with a different type of people.

A transfer came for us a year after my accident. We were sent to central Pennsylvania with the nearest RLDS Church a mission, sixty miles away; but we managed to attend almost every Sunday. I was baptized five months after we arrived. A few short months later my husband was called and ordained to the priesthood of our church.

And I did have an air embolism! The lung X ray proved this. The air did go into my bloodstream, heart, and brain. But I'm a healthy person today, seven years later. The only ill effects that I have are a slight "faint" feeling and shortness of breath when I recall the experience. The symptoms have been with me even while writing this testimony.

I have been told in a blessing by a patriarch in the church that "a guardian angel has been watching over you and caring for you personally. He, likewise, has been and still is watching over you and your loved ones. He will continue to watch over your life as you continue to dedicate yourself to the tasks of right living and service to your heavenly Father."

I come face-to-face with God often these days when I find that I have wandered away from "right living." I see his face, saddened, because of me; and I remember what he has done for me. He gave his life and then spared mine. Can I do less than serve him?

The Word Repentance

By Robert C. Skoor

My association with the church as a member started the summer of 1948. My mother and younger brother, John, were also baptized that day. Since that time the process of development around a Christ-centered life has gone forward with slow determination. I can then, with many others, state that the church has had an influence over my life from an early age.

I have had some experiences down through the years which I would term dramatic, but by and large it has been the slow, seemingly everyday things that have made the difference. Many individuals other than my parents extended to me the patience, love, and concern which at times I most certainly didn't deserve. Strong testimonies of how life should be lived were given by men and women of my home congregation with such effect that even though death has taken many of them I still remember their lives.

In a more universal way the testimony of Christ has been extended by World Church officials, and along with this the years at Graceland College. For many reasons my days at college were not the most pleasant of life's experiences to remember. But it was during those years that the message of Christ, the program of the church, and my place in it began to take shape. It was at Graceland that a most outstanding worship experience was mine. This I would like to share.

As a church member, I had been aware of the importance of the word repentance. I knew the attitudes which were akin to it such as humility, faith, and love. But until the spring of 1959, I can honestly say that the experience of true repentance had never been mine. I remember very clearly walking into the Student Center where the Easter sunrise service for 1959 was to be held. This particular service was being led by the senior class under the direction of Roy Cheville.

As the service progressed through the introductory stage, I kept thinking that everything was much the same as any other service and wished I had stayed in bed. At this point, however, the scripture message was read. I can still remember the scripture and the student who read it. The scripture was from the twenty-first chapter of John. The verses 15-17 hit home like nothing I had ever experienced before, even though I had read and heard them read many times.

> "So when they had dined, Jesus saith to Simon Peter, Simon, son of Jonas, lovest thou me more than these? He saith unto him, Yea, Lord; thou knowest that I love thee. He saith unto him, Feed my lambs."

These words were stated to Peter in much the same way three times. I recall that when the student finished reading verse 17 it seemed as though the Master of men had been speaking to me.

I saw my life at that moment in time for what it was—selfish and egocentric, with no underlying motive for its existence other than self-gratification. I left the building that morning a reoriented person.

The years that have passed have not diminished the desire made that day to feed the sheep of God. Through the lives of many committed people and the patient, ever flowing Spirit of Christ the call to serve has come to me.

I sincerely believe that when a man meets his Lord, attitudes, desires, and past expressions of life are reshaped. Since that day the church's ministry extended in preaching, teaching, and counseling has helped me continue the resolve I made that spring morning when the resurrected Christ spoke to the inner man.

The Hand of the Lord

By Cecil Robbins

Clarence Koller was employed as a pressman. One afternoon while operating his machine his foot slipped and he

175

automatically threw out his arm to break his fall. Suddenly his left hand was caught by the steel rollers of the printing press and pulled through. Fortunately the press girl on the other side of the rollers spotted the blood-stained paper and, realizing an accident had taken place, immediately shut off the machine. The rollers were set in bearings and casings of the bearings were bolted to the steel framework of the machine. These particular rollers were set at one-fourth inch. A machinist was summoned to unscrew the bearings from the steel structure in order that the rollers might be pried apart. Clarence did not faint, but helped to pry the rollers apart in order to free his hand. Five to ten minutes were consumed before the hand was freed.

The hand, being flattened to one-fourth inch, was virtually destroyed. Bones were crushed, tendons were torn and muscles were mutilated. Clarence said, "My hand looked like a thin, large hamburger." Clarence suffered no immediate pain. He did not want to alarm his wife, so requested that someone notify his daughter and inform her that he was being taken to Niagara Falls Memorial Hospital and that she should come as soon as possible.

After Clarence arrived at the hospital he was given heavy sedation. Two doctors checked the hand and, since little consultation seemed necessary, decided that the hand must be removed. The doctors were amazed, however, when in conference with his daughter she insisted—rather vehemently —that this not be done. The mutilated hand was placed in a banjo-type sling.

When the tragedy was brought to the attention of the pastor, Elder Clifford Spilsbury (who worked at the same plant), he went to administer to Clarence by the laying on of hands. That evening because of sedation it was difficult for Clarence's wife Ethel and others to convince him that the hand was still attached. Many prayers were offered by church members for Clarence.

After two weeks in the hospital Clarence was allowed to return home. The doctors insisted that the hand would eventually have to be amputated. They felt that the request to allow the hand to remain on the arm was very unreasonable.

While at home one day Clarence was lying on the bed facing the wall. He was both thinking and praying about his hand. Suddenly Clarence discovered that a most brilliant silvery light about the size of a pinhead had appeared on the wall. The tiny, brilliant light began to expand until the entire wall became a vast screen of light. In the midst of the light there appeared an arched doorway with one step leading to it. A most beautiful personage with a face resembling a painting of the head of Christ appeared in the doorway. He was dressed in a robe exquisitely white. The personage walked forward, placed his hand on the crushed hand of Clarence, and said, "Have no fear, your hand will be saved." Clarence felt the slight pressure of the hand placed over his and also a supreme joy of association with such a pure and kindly being. After the reassurance, the personage turned, walked up the step, and stepped through the doorway. The screen of light began to diminish in size until it once again became the size of a pinhead—and then disappeared. Clarence was left to rejoice and ponder over the singularity of such a wonderful blessing.

Over the next months there were hours of therapy for the hand, including massaging, manipulations, and exercises. This happened in 1953. Clarence is now seventy-six, has wonderful use of the hand, and experiences no adverse effects to climatic changes or hard usage. All of the normal feelings and sensations are present in the hand. Clarence said that he believes his daughter was influenced by the power of the Holy Spirit in her decision not to allow the amputation. When I asked Clarence about his hand he confided, "I often look at the hand and relive the experience when the Master applied the touch of his hand and told me to have no fear. I only hope that I can live so as finally to enjoy the constant companionship of One so great and good!"

When Neighbors Witness

By Bob and Portia Stanke

It had been raining steadily for seven days and nights. During our evening devotions, the children expressed concern for the families in the foothills and asked God to keep them safe. A devastating August fire had denuded the Glendora and Azusa foothills of all ground cover. And now the rains were causing grave concern to those families along the base of the foothills. We had no concern for ourselves or our neighborhood, for we had been assured by flood control officials that our area was safe. But it had rained so much that Tani wanted to hear about Noah and the ark so she and Mark could make all the animal sounds for baby Laura.

We retired for the night in the warm security of our home only to be awakened by Laura's restless crying at 5:30 a.m. We lay awake for a half hour aware that we were receiving a thundering, abnormal deluge of rain. Suddenly we were jolted by a frightening sound—a strange, loud, echoing roar. Bob was up with a shout. Black mud was pouring through the wall air-conditioner into our bedroom. Through the sliding glass doors in the living room we could see mud and debris rapidly filling the backyard and tearing through trees and foliage. "Get the children, we have to get out right now!" Bob shouted. Three pairs of arms were upraised. There were no sleepy protests, no questions why. The front door crashed in and we turned to see a five-foot wall of glass, mud, boulders, and branches crush through the sliding glass doors in front of which Bob had stood just seconds before. Barefoot and in our night clothes, we worked through a raging river of mud to the car parked in the driveway. In seconds, the entire house was filled with wall-to-wall mud, four feet deep. Boulders and branches shattered and buried our furniture.

We sat in the car with a river of mud and household goods rushing past us. We remained surprisingly calm—there was no terror or panic. Bob led us as we quietly prayed together that the rain would stop and we would be safe. As daylight approached the rain ended. Neighbors welcomed us into the warmth of their home. We were thankful to be unharmed and together as a family.

Mark, with tears in his eyes, said so soberly after seeing the damage, "Dad, I'm never, never going to be bad again, so God won't send any more mud." We had explained during our worship the night before that God sent the flood during Noah's time because the people were wicked. Now how could we explain that what had occurred to us was not a like punishment? We felt that words would not convince Mark, but hoped that by witnessing and experiencing God's love as expressed through people and events, he might understand. That which transpired in the days and weeks to follow all but convinced him and reaffirmed our faith in a loving, caring heavenly Father who withholds nothing that is needful from his children.

That day and the days which followed belong to the wonderful people of the city of Azusa. They came in waves, with hot food, shovels, and hoses. Men took days off from work to help. School students, strangers for the most part, and housewives we had never met, labored from early morning until daylight had vanished—in pouring rain and biting cold. Neighbors left their own muddy yards and spent days assisting us in saving our belongings. People gave of themselves, freely and without ceasing. It was a true and living testimony of the goodness and compassion in the hearts of people.

We were in need of temporary shelter. We feel that God provided the loving home of members of our church group. To the children, the American Red Cross was to the Stankes what the ark was to Noah. This organization provided immediate attention and financial help for clothing. At a cost of about $1,700 they moved and stored our salvageable possessions, found us a home for five months through FHA that was rent free, and financially assisted us in furnishing the home with items that were most essential.

In the days which followed we were physically exhausted several times. At times it seemed impossible that we could lift one more shovel of mud or face one more decision. In these periods we raised our voices in prayer and repeatedly received strength to our aching limbs, clarity of tightened thought, and peace of spirit.

In retrospect, we are grateful to have been directed to that particular house and neighborhood four years earlier. We had asked God to lead us to a neighborhood and congregation where we could best serve him, and received the assurance that this was where he would have us serve. Bob was an elder in the Reorganized Church of Jesus Christ of Latter Day Saints and had accepted the responsibility to be the pastor of the Covina congregation. In our court of eight families where we lived there was need for ministry. Two young mothers of the group had died within a month of each other, one because of illness, the other by suicide. After the deaths, there were five children left bewildered and lost without their mothers. We had been close to these families, sharing our love and encouraging them. How thankful we were to have been where God could use us to love and care for these little ones through those difficult months.

We have never for a moment considered the mud slide to be a disaster nor do we feel we have suffered any great loss materially. The biggest loss was the inconvenience and delay. We were blessed in escaping death in the slide. We have been blessed by experiencing the love and sacrifice of people in concrete ways. We have seen our family unite and grow in faith and strength. We have felt each day direction, sustained strength, and a peace of mind and soul—a gift of our heavenly Father. We can only be grateful for life's experiences that have brought out the best in us and others. The rich blessings that have come far outweigh and diminish what we have lost materially. We have never felt sorrow, bitterness, or futility. There have been no tears shed, but instead there has been much good humor, laughter, and moments of true joy as others have shared with us. The first comment of one of the priesthood members of our church as he entered our muddy home with shovel in hand was "Portia, you're the sloppiest housekeeper I've ever seen." My reply was, "John, did you wipe your feet?" Out of this experience has come many testimonies of the power of God at work in our lives.

Our seven-year-old Mark commented recently, "There's one thing I *really* know 'for sure' about God, Mom. He likes me enough to help me when I ask him." That simple affirmation sums up the abiding truth that is the foundation of our faith as a family. We believe assuredly that God is, that he cares for us, he reveals his will, and directs our lives in a most personal way.

We are more obviously aware of the power of God in times of peril or great personal need. It is then that we willingly place our lives in his hands. He is, however, just as concerned, just as willing to direct and lead us all the days of our lives. Nothing is too big or too small, no period of time too calm or troubled not to approach our heavenly Father. His power, strength, and wisdom are available to us if we but ask, humbly recognizing our need for his help in all aspects of our lives. How could we possibly feel other than richly blessed by a loving heavenly Father who constantly reveals his will and directs the lives of his children?

Jesus Christ Created Me

By Akihiko Taira

I was born in Manchuria in 1940. At the end of World War II some Japanese were taken to Russia by the Soviet Army. Others, including my family, were imprisoned in North Korea. For two and one-half years I was the only Japanese boy in a North Korean Communist school. Just before the Korean War my family and other Japanese nationals, for reasons unknown to us, were force-marched to the Thirty-eighth Parallel by the North Korean Army. There we were released and moved south to Seoul, where we lived for one year.

In 1951 my family were privileged finally to return to our homeland in Japan. Due to financial reasons I had to leave my home in Hyogo Prefecture (near Osaka) when I was a senior high school student to live with my father's relatives in Okinawa. I completed high school in Okinawa, and went on to graduate from the Ryukyu University where I had majored in business administration. It was while I was a student at the university that I found the restored church.

I was amazed—and my soul rejoiced—at the teachings of Jesus Christ. The gospel preached was most simple and very easy to understand. I felt as if I were being "soaked" in it. I had thought that obtaining an understanding of life and truth would be most difficult without special academic and scholarly study in philosophy, religion, and science. However, after my introduction to the gospel I realized that it was the Holy Spirit which leads men to understand truth or, in other words, life and the meaning of life. The Spirit kindly led the way to the place where my soul would find rest.

I accepted the teachings of Jesus Christ in their beauty and simplicity. I was baptized two weeks after I first met the "Lord of Life." In Christ I found the source and the beginning of my life. That Jesus Christ created me was the greatest discovery! It was He who had sovereignty and authority over my destiny. Ultimate salvation was available only in Jesus Christ—not in Buddha, great philosophies, the teaching of parents, tradition, or the power of the state.

My soul thrilled with this revelation of God's love and concern for me, and my heart was filled with gratitude to the minister who first introduced me to my Creator.

Before I met the Lord Jesus I was a helpless atheist—believing that my existence was due to a natural law over which I had no control but which law had absolute control over me. I cried and cursed my lot. I hated my parents who had brought me into a world in which I must suffer and die for no purpose. At times I felt it would have been better if I had never been born. On other occasions I was ashamed because I didn't have the courage to take my own life. I was most miserable.

Imagine the joy that flooded my soul when I first met the Master and discovered that I was not a creature of accident! It was not my parents through some unfeeling natural law that had given me life but Christ—in whom "all things were made." I had found my true Creator!

In 1965 I had an opportunity to go to the United States on a scholarship. During the eighteen months in the States I had the privilege of fellowshiping with the Saints in many places. As a result, my testimony of the Restoration gospel matured greatly.

In the body of Christ I have found my life's purpose and goal. I testify that for the first time in my life I have shared in true brotherhood—a relationship in which I am genuinely needed, and in which I am learning to truly rely on others. This is the first time I have really felt that I know the meaning of the word "need." It was *in* the body of Christ—the fellowship of the Saints—that I made this great discovery.

Before I encountered the restored church I was always skeptical when Christians talked about the existence of the "mystical" body of Christ on earth. However, by the grace of God, I found his church and, thus, discovered this "body." The church was not a building, or a seminary school, or an association of scholars discussing metaphysical ideology. No, the body of Christ—the church—is comprised of ordinary men and women, youth and children who meet Jesus every day and in every way in their lives, and are hence associated together in "body" relationship. I am deeply grateful to be a part of this "body," and my sincere prayer is that the countless millions in my part of the world who are crying out in darkness and despair will respond to the Spirit—as I did—and meet him who creates and sustains all, Jesus Christ.

Behold, You Have Not Understood

By John Moffett

I am a fourth-generation Latter Day Saint. I came into the church because of my parents. During my late teens, I entertained certain doubts about my membership. I didn't want to belong to a church merely because of inheritance. This question became all the more disturbing as we sang the song "Give Me That Old Time Religion" in a light vein during a Zion's League youth activity. One of the lines of the song reads, "If it's good enough for Granddad, it's good enough for me." I didn't feel that because it was good enough for Granddad it was necessarily good enough for me. But my parents were good, active church members; I didn't want to hurt or disturb them by telling them of my doubts.

But I had to resolve my doubts. I began by reviewing the history of the church from its beginning. I reasoned that if Joseph Smith had angelic visitors, why shouldn't I. This would convince me, and I would put all questions aside. Like Joseph Smith I retreated alone into our peach orchard in California. There, in a secluded location, I poured my heart out to God. I prayed and prayed, but no answer came. Neither did I receive my spectacular experience.

Later, Brother Charles Hield, an apostle of the church, was in our area and preached a sermon, using a text taken from the ninth section of the Doctrine and Covenants, one of the books of the church. As he read, the words seemed to leap out to me.

"Behold, you have not understood; you have supposed that I would give it unto you, when you took

185

no thought, save it was to ask me; but behold, I say unto you, that you must study it out in your mind; then you must ask me if it be right, and if it is right, I will cause that your bosom shall burn within you; therefore, you shall feel that it is right; but if it be not right, you shall have no such feelings, but you shall have a stupor of thought."

These words struck home. At the time this revelation was given in 1829, the message was for Oliver Cowdery on a different matter, but these words seemed to counsel me on the method of receiving communication from God through prayer.

I put the scriptural insight to a test, and my mind was impressed with these words; not in an audible, spectacular way, but none the less real: "My son, if I had given you the kind of experience you requested, it would not have been for your best good. You would have become satisfied, having only one testimony. By experimenting upon my words as contained in the scriptures, you may have many testimonies. By and by the pieces of my gospel and purposes will fit together, and you will understand and be convinced."

This promise has been fulfilled. I am convinced as to the divinity of this work, not because it was good enough for Dad, Granddad, and Great-granddad but because I have my own testimony of many experiences which have caused me to believe and know. I am grateful for my inheritance in the church because through this medium I have received knowledge of the gospel. I am more thankful for the fact that our faith stands on a greater rock than tradition. Those who are honest in heart may find their searching rewarded with truth as our heavenly Father seeks to reveal himself and his purposes to all mankind.

The Love of Christ

By Etienne P. Vanaa

I was born on the island of Rangiroa which is located about two hundred miles northeast of the main island of Tahiti. I was raised in a divided home; my father was RLDS and my mother a strong and devout Catholic. I remember when I was a very little boy that she used to take me to her church every evening and every Sunday. And in the evening she taught me to pray. When I was older, I used to go to the church by myself. I do not know why I went to the church every Sunday, but I knew that it was my duty to go more than anything else.

We were not a rich family. My father was a copra farmer who had to work hard in order to meet the needs of our family of six. I was the oldest in the family which consists of myself, two brothers, and one sister.

When I reached the age of ten, my family moved to the main island of Tahiti in order to send us to school. My mother found a job with a very low income that permitted us to settle in our new surroundings, little by little.

After our move to Tahiti, I was sent until the year of 1948 to the *Ecole des Freres* with two of my brothers. In this year my mother died and we were left alone with my father, who worked as a sailor on a small schooner in order to support his family. I was then, if I remember correctly, twelve years of age. Fortunately, with that providential care of our heavenly Father, my grandfather, Hamau Faana, came to see my father. He volunteered to take one of the children under his care. Grandfather, the father of my father, was then the Mission yard caretaker of the Reorganized Latter

187

Day Saints on Tahiti. He was also an elder in the church. I was selected to make my home with him.

I was never forced to attend any RLDS services. I did not want to go, but I knew that he wanted me to attend. I refused his invitation many times and yet I felt his love and concern. He was patient and humble enough in trying to understand a grandson such as I.

One evening, after having been in his home for a while and while we were having supper together, he asked me if I would be interested in attending youth activities. I said that I was. He replied that the young people of the church were going to have their weekly meeting that night and that it would be a good idea just to go and see. I decided to go but, of course, with some reservations. Eugene Huioutu, our next-door neighbor, came to get me and together we went to the meeting. He was very friendly and so were all the young people that I met for the first time. After the meeting we had games, fun, and refreshments. I thought over and over again of the friendliness, love, and concern of those young people. I was really impressed. A few weeks later, I felt again that love among them, and I knew that they had something I did not have. That love, that concern, that friendliness I had not found among my other friends.

This was the starting point of a new direction in my life. I had found the real love of Christ; I decided to involve myself in every activity of the young people, and with the help and guidance of my grandfather I was able to see more clearly the message of this church. Little by little he introduced me to the teachings of the church. He told me the story of a young man by the name of Joseph Smith. He told me of the love of God and about his Son, the Christ. Finally, I was ready to join the church. It was not easy, but I knew that this was the church of Jesus Christ.

After my conversion into the restored church, I became

very active. My grandfather helped me to continue my education and he has helped me to become a knowledgeable Reorganized Latter Day Saint. Before he died these were his last words for me: "Etienne, the greatest desire that I have for you is that someday you become a servant for the Lord." Those words still resound in my mind today because they had meaning, and the meaning has become a reality.

I am grateful to my mother who led me into the fellowship of Christian saints. I am grateful to my grandfather who gave me the love and the truthfulness of the Church of Jesus Christ. But above all I am grateful to my heavenly Father for his continuous care, love, and guidance during my early existence.

Today I can testify that He lives because I have the assurance of his love and his care. I know that he loves the Polynesian people as well as he loves people of other countries. Because he lives, and because of this testimony, all the members of my family have joined the church.

It is my desire to continue to serve Him to the best of my ability wherever I may be. This is my prayer and my testimony.

This Is God's Work

By George B. Franklin

As a boy I was reared in a home divided in religion. My mother was of the Catholic faith and my father was a Presbyterian. I attended both churches as a youth. Later during my high school years I became acquainted with a young Lutheran minister who was a neighbor. He was interested in sports, and since I was "center" on the high school basketball team, he attended many of the games and often furnished my transportation.

I learned to love this young minister because he was willing to listen to my concern about religion. He answered many of the questions which neither my mother nor my father could answer. I became interested in the church he represented and after receiving instructions and learning the catechism was baptized into the Lutheran Church. I felt I had solved my religious problem. I was in the "middle of the road"—neither Catholic nor Presbyterian but near enough to both to be satisfied.

Then I met a girl who was a member of a church with a strange name, the Reorganized Church of Jesus Christ of Latter Day Saints. Later this girl and I were married and we moved to another city. I transferred my church membership and my wife's was transferred for her, but neither of us attended church services for some time in the new city. I later attended services at my church and tried to induce my companion to attend with me. I painted a picture for her of the nice pipe organ, the robed choir, the lovely altar and church building, but these made no impression upon her. It then became quite easy for me not to attend also. Later that year we learned the location of the Reorganized Church, but we attended no church services in spite of the fact that across the street from our home was a Presbyterian Church and not too far away was a Lutheran Church—as well as my wife's church.

One evening upon arriving home from work my companion said to me, "I had a visitor today."

I asked, "Who was it?"

"Your minister," she replied.

When I inquired as to the purpose of his call she informed me that among other things he was interested in our contributing to the church. She told him, "I contribute to my church and my companion can do likewise to his." My pastor then asked to what church my wife belonged, and when she told him the Reorganized Church of Jesus Christ of Latter Day Saints he said, "Oh, you are one of those things." This was disturbing to me and I replied that if that was the way he felt about my wife's religion, I would not go back to the church again but would attend with her.

I then began to read the literature of the RLDS Church, especially the Book of Mormon which up to this time lay on a stand untouched by me but often read by my companion. After I started to read it I could not put it down and was influenced greatly as I read. Never before had such a wonderful feeling come over me, and every time I studied the book something kept telling me, "This is God's work."

One night I had a dream. In it I was attending a church service. It was not the church to which I belonged nor was I sure it was the one to which my companion belonged, but I saw three ministers mount the rostrum as the services began. I was amused at the minister sitting in the center. He was short, rather plump, and wore a neatly trimmed goatee. He read from the Book of Isaiah which spoke of a book coming forth and he held up the book—the very book I had been reading, the Book of Mormon. I awoke rather happily, but disturbed, and asked myself why I hadn't put the scripture and the book together as did this minister. Then I dismissed the dream from my mind. I continued to study the church and presently I joined.

One Sunday during church school I noticed that our teacher smiled rather pleasantly at someone who came in late. My former training relative to church behavior kept me from turning around, but I was curious. When the class session was over I deliberately changed my seat so I could take a quick glance at the latecomer. To my astonishment there was the man I had seen in my dream, the man with a neatly trimmed goatee. He was to be the guest speaker for that morning's service. I was fascinated by his appearance and delivery. Here was a revelation. I knew the church was founded upon revelation. Now my conviction of its truthfulness was verified by revelation. I was sure our heavenly Father was revealing to me through my dream and the visit of his servant that this was the true church of Jesus Christ. The man was Gomer T. Griffiths, once an apostle, but to me a revealer that "God works in mysterious ways his wonders to perform."

Three years later I was ordained a priest. Three years after that I became an elder. I served as pastor for fifteen years. I was a district president for sixteen years and during this time I was ordained a high priest. Later I was ordained an evangelist and patriarch.

I know this is Christ's church. I have seen his power manifest through the ordinance of administration to the sick. I have heard his voice speak to his people and the Spirit has borne witness that God is alive, ready and willing to assist all who in humility will ask of him.

The Spirit of God has been my stay and my guide and has made me seek to develop into the kind of individual he intended me to be. I am grateful to the church for making this a possibility.

I Thank My God

By Rosie Sellers

In 1936 my mother and father developed a close association with some friends who were members of the

RLDS Church. Within a year of this friendship and after attending a series given by the missionary to Germany, Johan Smolney, they were baptized. My father was very happy with his new church and attended every service even though he was rejected by some of his family and friends.

In 1939 World War II began in Germany and my father was one of the first who had to join the Army. He was stationed in various countries and later was a part of the German Army that went to Russia.

On October 4, 1941, he was killed in Russia. It is not hard to remember the day when the postman handed my mother the telegram which told of my father's death. Countless tears flowed down her cheeks at that time. She knew of the responsibilities that faced her. She had three little children and one who was still a baby to worry about.

The war was still with my family. No one knew from one day to the next if a bomb would hit the house. Almost every night the town was awakened by sirens. My mother rushed her children to the bunkers with a little candle in each child's hand. At times my mother would kneel in prayer through the entire night and pray to God for peace and protection—and her children would gather around her and listen. On many mornings when the townspeople came out of the bunkers, buildings would be burning and the screams of the wounded were heard. Still my family did not lose its hope and faith in God that he would keep it safe and protected.

A couple of months after my father's death, my mother had a beautiful dream. In her dream she saw my father dressed in his uniform and he told her to stay in this church because it was the truth. The dream meant a lot to my mother and it always gave her faith and confidence in those dark days of the terrible war.

In 1942 I started to school in the first grade. It seemed to me that I spent more hours in the bunkers than I spent in the classroom. One day during my half-hour walk to school the sirens were sounded. I could not return home so I sought shelter in a streetcar stop. Bombs fell all around me but I came out safe and went on to school. In 1944 my mother left me with friends out in the country for protection—so I would not have to take part in the Hitler Youth Marches.

In 1945 the war finally came to an end. American soldiers came to my town. They came into my family's apartment looking for all sorts of things and after they completed their search of the house they took my mother and others on their truck to get their passes changed. I remember the terrible feeling I had when I saw my mother on that truck and I didn't know if I would ever see her again. There I stood with one hand on my little brother and the other on my little sister and all of us were crying. I was relieved when my mother returned home later that day.

The war was now over but the pain remained. Many people were homeless and food was rationed. Sometimes there was not enough bread on the table to feed all of us. Many times some of my family went on an all-day bike trip out to beg for a piece of bread from a farmer or, if really lucky, an egg.

On top of the other troubles, in 1947 my mother was thrown off her bicycle when hit by a truck. The doctors thought she would die that night, but I trusted in Jesus and prayed all night. The next day I went to an elder and asked him to go and see Mother in the hospital to administer to her. She remained in the hospital for four months before she came home.

It was during these four months that we received several CARE packages from church members in Independence, Missouri. They meant a lot to us, especially the food. They were an answer to a prayer.

In February 1960 I met my husband. At that time he was not a member of my church. In fact, before entering the Army he had completed three and one-half years of college preparing to become a minister in another church. The first year of marriage was not a very happy time, for he wanted me to give up my church. There were many sad and miserable days, for feelings were strong. I was told that if I would not stop going to my church the marriage would end in divorce. Once again, as through the war years, there was nothing else for me to do except kneel beside my bed and pray to my God to let me be strong.

Then in October 1961 I begged him to go with me to the RLDS Retreat in Berchtesgaden. Following this experience he told me he was sorry for every unpleasant thing he had said about my church. After several meetings with Brother Peter Harder he was baptized in May 1962. Since then he has been ordained to the office of priest and is now active in the branch at Offenbach.

I thank my God for all the blessings he has granted me and for his wonderful church which has meant so much to me and my family. It shall be my desire always to serve him in any way that I can for the rest of my life.

Compelled to Climb

By Betty L. Seagraves

I awakened quickly following the dream. A cold awareness had come over me, and I reached over and shook my husband. "I've had the strangest dream," I said as he struggled from his sleep.

"If you had a strange dream," he grumbled sleepily, "it only means you shouldn't have eaten those pickles before you went to bed last night."

Of course I should have known that he would brush off the experience so easily. My husband's ridicule of my early spiritual beliefs came back to me vividly, and I remembered my almost-too-eager willingness to relinquish them.

I had married at the age of fifteen; he had been twenty-five, and now nearly fifteen years later I looked back on a run-of-the-mill marriage with the mill running less and less as the years rolled by.

There were, as a result of this marriage, three children whose entire religious training had been in the hands of Boy Scout, Brownie, and Girl Scout leaders. I drank (moderately) and smoked (excessively)—and avoided with care anything of a spiritual nature; and while the dream seemed to spark some remote emotion within me, my husband's rebuff quickly extinguished any ensuing flames. I immediately put it from my mind without awakening any of the long-forgotten emotions of the past.

There was, however, one emotion that had carried over from my youth, the love and respect I had for my father. Dad was a "preacher" when I was a little girl, but it had been a long time since either Dad or I had attended church. It was a surprise to me when the phone rang a few days later and my father approached me with a strange request.

"Betty," he said almost apologetically, "I had a call today from a young man I used to know. I was a young missionary when he was a little boy, and we were neighbors. You were a baby, but he and your sisters were playmates." Dad paused. "He is coming to town for a week-long preaching series. He asked me to attend and to see if you and your sisters would come with me."

"Well, . . ." I said hesitantly.

"It would mean a lot to me," Dad said.

"Oh, all right," I said in an irritated manner, "but I won't promise to go every night." Good grief, I thought, a whole week of church!

The man who was preaching was Apostle Reed Holmes. As I sat in the church the first night he spoke, the futility of my life was flung suddenly before my face, and I remembered with tremendous impact the dream of several nights before. In my dream I had returned to the home of my childhood and was eagerly exploring the big old rambling house. In my dream, as I approached the stairs leading to the attic I felt compelled to climb. I placed my foot on the bottom step and voices shouted out at me. "No! No! Don't go up there. The stairs are steep and dangerous."

"But," I replied, more eager than ever, "when I was a child I hid all my broken and discarded toys up there. I want to see if they're still there."

"No! No!" the voices called again. "All those things are of no value. The past is dead. Let it lie."

"I must climb the stairs," I said, and started up.

The climb was difficult. Cobwebs had to be brushed aside, rodents sometimes scrambled over my feet frightening me, but at last I reached the top. I peeked through the door, cautiously at first; then in exhilaration I flung the attic door open wide. There, row after beautiful row, I beheld tables laden with new and shining treasure. Things of a temporal nature to be sure, but items I sorely needed in my present life. "Look," I said to the voices, "I thought these things of no value, but what is here will fill my every need . . ." and then I awoke in the cold assurance that the dream meant something special.

I now awoke spiritually in the service, and over me surged the assurance that this church I had so easily abandoned not only meant something but was indeed that very stabilizing force I lacked in my chaotic life.

For a moment I was beseiged by fears. Would God forgive me for those wasted years? Could I find strength to hold fast to the truth in spite of my companion's attitude? And then came that wonderful peace of God's forgiving and the knowledge that with his help I could hold to that which I knew to be true.

It wasn't always an easy climb, but like the stairs to the attic it was a rewarding one. As I reexamined the doctrine of Christ and applied it to my life the very fiber of my being changed and with it my home and family relations. In a few months my two teen-age children were baptized. In less than three years I stood at the water's edge and watched my husband embrace the gospel. Three years later he and our son, David, sat side by side as hands were laid upon their heads to ordain them members of God's holy priesthood. I have often wondered where and what we would be had not God reached out and invited me back.

There have been unnumbered blessings and joys during these years. There have been trials, too, but through them has come a new and greater strength. I have developed a greater assurance and testimony of Jesus Christ and his church. But most of all has come the knowledge of the great love that God has for all of his children. Yes, a love so great that it reaches out for even such as I.

The Only Satisfaction

By Shelly Stevens

As a boy I lived on a farm in the state of Arkansas. My father was three-fourths Cherokee Indian, dedicated, sincere, and devoted to his family. My mother was also part Indian and they worked together; yet we could not afford any luxuries, not even a toy or Christmas candy. My father died when I was seven years old and I was sent to a home for orphans in Little Rock.

My earliest ambitions were like those of any orphan. Because I never had a toy of my own, and because I looked longingly at the candy bars I couldn't buy, I wanted to make money—lots of it. In a way, this was a good thing; at least it served as motivation for "going on to school" when otherwise I might have been content to end my education with a high school diploma. I learned all I could in the field of electricity, and when World War II began I took a job as foreman in a plant. After the war I started my own business, and soon I was able to buy all the things that I had ever wished for. What surprised me was that they did not bring the happiness I had anticipated.

Shortly after Mildred and I were married we began attending one of the large Protestant churches in Detroit—the same denomination I had affiliated with as a boy. I was no more impressed by the services then than I had been in my youth, so one Sunday Mildred suggested that we attend her church (up to this time she had never mentioned her religious beliefs). The appearance of the meeting place was something of a shock—an Odd Fellows Hall much in need of paint. However, inside I felt a warmth and "belongingness" I had never experienced before. After the service I even stayed to help the other men in the congregation fold up the chairs and stack them. As we left that battered building, I turned to Mildred and said, "I want to be a part of this."

The following year I was baptized, and the congregation moved into a new building—the Redford Church. I began studying the Three Standard Books and found the Doctrine

199

and Covenants especially appealing. Despite my interest in this newfound religion, I was completely surprised when the presiding elder told me of my call to the priesthood (actually I had only a vague idea of what priesthood was). I did not accept because I felt I had so little to offer, and I wasn't sure that I ever would have the necessary qualifications. I did, however, agree to pray about the matter. Several weeks later, as I was resting one evening, an illumined message appeared before me: "Time will qualify you." I knew this had to be more than my imagination, because it was not the sort of manifestation I would have dreamed up myself. When the pastor next asked me if I would reconsider the call, I told him I would accept. I was ordained a priest in 1959 and six years later an elder.

Since my affiliation with the church—and especially since becoming a minister—I have found life rich beyond anything money can buy. I know from experience that material wealth cannot satisfy a starving soul. For me, the message and mission of Christ bring the only lasting satisfaction life can offer.

My experiences since becoming a member of the church convince me that Joseph Smith, Jr., was a prophet of God, and that God is articulate. At the very center of the Restoration movement is the remarkable proclamation, "This is my beloved Son; hear ye him."

My personal relationship to these facts sustains my enthusiasm and motivates me in my intensive search for knowledge to become a competent, self-authenticating base of Christlike influence, to become strategically involved in social relationships, to impress upon all who come within range of my influence the spirit and intent of our Lord, Jesus Christ.

I find my greatest joy in witnessing whether in preaching or talking to an individual about the gospel. I especially like

to share the good news with the lonely and poor, because
—remembering my own unhappy youth and my misguided
ambition—I know that I have something to give them that
will make their lives lastingly rich.

A Firsthand Experience

By Carl Cederstrom

The only thing I knew about the "Mormons" was that
which I had learned in an American history course. I thought
they had all moved to Utah during the exodus from the
Midwest. My introduction to the church came when I met
the girl who was to become my wife. As our courtship
progressed to the point that I wanted to propose marriage, I
asked Verna to what church she belonged. I was not a
faithful church attender, but I considered myself as good a
Christian as anyone else. I also knew that unity in the religion
of husband and wife was one of the basic ingredients to a
happy and successful marriage. When she said, "I belong to
the Reorganized Church of Jesus Christ of Latter Day
Saints," I said, "Oh, you mean the 'Mormon' church." That
was the beginning of my introduction to the restored gospel,
as I was quickly informed of the differences between the
Reorganized Latter Day Saints and the group that had
headquarters in Utah.

In the months that followed I read parts of the Book of
Mormon and attended church services with her. My feelings
ran the gamut from outright doubt to complete belief and
back again. Having been reared in a popular Protestant

church, many of the hazy beliefs which I held were exposed to close and often uncomfortable scrutiny. On the other hand, I found that certain questions I had had concerning baptism and prophetic guidance were answered completely. At the age of eight weeks I had been baptized (christened) in my church. The event had had no particular meaning for me, as I was not conscious of it nor was it of my own volition. In the back of my mind kept running the scripture, "Repent and be baptized." At eight weeks of age I had not repented of anything.

Also, for a number of years I had wondered why God had ceased speaking to his people. Why no more scripture after Christ's ministry on earth? Not being a deep Bible scholar or theological thinker, I did not know how or where to look for the answers. Even though I wondered about these things, I was unprepared for the good news that God does reveal himself today and does continue to guide and direct his church.

After our romance had blossomed into marriage we moved into a house two blocks from Second Church in Independence, Missouri. Every Sunday morning Verna would go to church school while I would "drift" to church for the preaching service. After all, I reasoned, Sunday school was for kids. After about a month of this I came to the conclusion that I didn't like walking up to the church alone and I was sure Verna didn't either. So we started going to church school together.

In the class I received a firsthand experience of the restored gospel working in the lives of people. The young adult class at the church was composed largely of men and women who had grown up in the congregational area, gone to school together, attended Zion's League youth meetings and camps and reunions together, and had even married within the group. Here I was, a total stranger and a nonmember. Yet

I was welcomed and accepted as if I too had been one of them all through the years. We were included in all of the activities, planned and spontaneous. I was impressed with their wholesome approach to life and their high spiritual tone. Their friendly concern for me—combined with the knowledge gained through the church school classes—convinced me that I wanted to taste of this fruit most precious, the restored gospel of Jesus Christ.

I was so converted to the gospel, even before baptism, that when the missionary coordinator, Glen Stewart, invited me to attend cottage meetings at another nonmember's house, my thought was, Glen wants me to help him convert that fellow.

I was baptized at Second Church on April 18, 1954. At the time of my baptism I was on active duty in the Navy, and my outlook on life was, "What's in it for me?" Since that time I have grown to realize that God has a purpose for each one to fulfill. Thanks to the influences of the Holy Spirit in my life I have seen that I should give as I am able rather than take. I have had the steady assurance that my life has been directed by my heavenly Father. There have been moments of his overwhelming Spirit. More important has been the sustaining, quiet, day-to-day influence guiding my thoughts and actions.